Ruth McEnery Stuart

Moriah's Mourning, and other half-hour Sketches

Ruth McEnery Stuart

Moriah's Mourning, and other half-hour Sketches

ISBN/EAN: 9783743348769

Manufactured in Europe, USA, Canada, Australia, Japa

Cover: Foto ©ninafisch / pixelio.de

Manufactured and distributed by brebook publishing software (www.brebook.com)

Ruth McEnery Stuart

Moriah's Mourning, and other half-hour Sketches

L.E.FROST.

"'THANK THE LORD! NOW I CAN SEE TO LOOK FOR 'EM!'"

MORIAH'S MOURNING

and Other Half-Hour Sketches

By **RUTH McENERY STUART**

Author of "In Simpkinsville"

"A Golden Wedding" etc.

WITH ILLUSTRATIONS

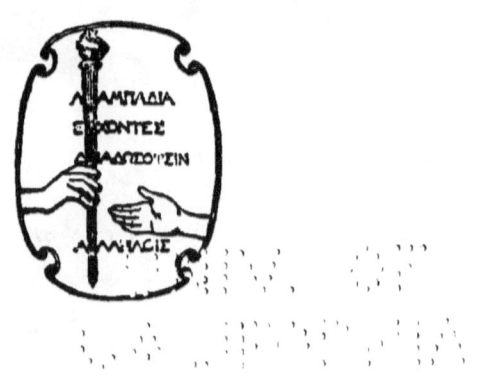

NEW YORK AND LONDON

HARPER & BROTHERS PUBLISHERS

CONTENTS

PAGE

MORIAH'S MOURNING 3

AN OPTICAL DILEMMA 19

THE SECOND MRS. SLIMM 37

APOLLO BELVEDERE. A CHRISTMAS EPISODE OF
THE PLANTATION 53

NEAREST OF KIN. (ON THE PLANTATION) 71

THE DEACON'S MEDICINE 93

TWO GENTLEMEN OF LEISURE 113

THE REV. JORDAN WHITE'S THREE GLANCES . . . 131

LADY. A MONOLOGUE OF THE COW-PEN 157

A PULPIT ORATOR 165

AN EASTER SYMBOL. A MONOLOGUE OF THE PLAN-
TATION 175

CHRISTMAS AT THE TRIMBLES' 181

A MINOR CHORD 211

ILLUSTRATIONS

"'THANK THE LORD ! *NOW I CAN SEE TO LOOK
FOR 'EM !*'" . . . . *Frontispiece*

"A SURPRISED AND SMILING MAN WAS SIT-
TING AT HER POLISHED KITCHEN TABLE" *Facing p.* 8

"'I'M AC–CHILLY MOST AFEERD *TO* SEE YOU
CONVERTED'". . . . .   "   40

"'I PROMISED HIM I'D PUT ON MO'NIN' FOR
HER SOON AS I MARRIED INTO DE
FAMILY'" . . . .   "   74

"SAYS SHE, 'OPEN YORE MOUTH !' AN' OF
CO'SE I OPENED IT" . . . .   "   98

"I DES LETS 'EM LOOSE P'OMISKYUS, TELL
EV'YBODY SEE BLUE LIGHTNIN'" . . .   "   134

"SALVATION'S KYAR IS MOVIN' !" . . . .   "   148

"'WON'T YER, PLEASE, SIR, SPELL DAT WORD
OUT FUR ME SLOW ?'". . . . . . .   "   168

MORIAH'S MOURNING

MORIAH'S MOURNING

M ORIAH was a widow of a month, and when she announced her intention of marrying again, the plantation held its breath. Then it roared with laughter.

Not because of the short period of her mourning was the news so incredible. But by a most exceptional mourning Moriah had put herself upon record as the most inconsolable of widows.

So prompt a readjustment of life under similar conditions was by no means unprecedented in colored circles.

The rules governing the wearing of the mourning garb are by no means stringent in plantation communities, and the widow who for reasons of economy or convenience sees fit to wear out her colored garments during her working hours is not held to account for so doing if she appear at all public functions clad in such weeds as she

may find available. It is not even needful, indeed, that her supreme effort should attain any definite standard. Anybody can collect a few black things, and there is often an added pathos in the very incongruity of some of the mourning toilettes that pass up the aisles of the colored churches.

Was not the soul of artlessness expressed in the first mourning of a certain young widow, for instance, who sewed upon her blue gown all the black trimming she could collect, declaring that she "would 'a' dyed de frock th'oo an' th'oo 'cep'n' it would 'a' swunked it up too much"? And perhaps her sympathetic companions were quite as *naïve* as she, for, as they aided her in these first hasty stitches, they poured upon her wounded spirit the healing oil of full and sympathetic approval, as the following remarks will testify.

"Dat frock mo'ns all right, now de black bows is on it."

"You kin put any colored frock in mo'nin' 'cep'n' a red one. Sew black on red, an' it laughs in yo' face."

"I'm a-sewin' de black fringe on de josey, Sis Jones, 'case fringe hit mo'ns a heap mo'nfuler 'n ribbon do."

4

Needless to say, a license so full and free as this found fine expression in a field of flowering weeds quite rare and beautiful to see.

Moriah had proven herself in many ways an exceptional person even before the occasion of her bereavement, and in this, contrary to all precedent, she had rashly cast her every garment into the dye-pot, sparing not even so much as her underwear.

Moriah was herself as black as a total eclipse, tall, angular, and imposing, and as she strode down the road, clad in the sombre vestments of sorrow, she was so noble an expression of her own idea that as a simple embodiment of dignified surrender to grief she commanded respect.

The plantation folk were profoundly impressed, for it had soon become known that her black garb was not merely a thing of the surface.

"Moriah sho' does mo'n for Numa. She mo'ns f'om de skin out." Such was popular comment, although it is said that one practical sister, to whom this "inward mo'nin'" had little meaning, ventured so far as to protest against it.

"Sis Moriah," she said, timidly, as she sat waiting while Moriah dressed for church—"Sis Moriah, look ter me like you'd be 'feerd dem black shimmies 'd draw out some sort o' tetter on yo' skin," to which bit of friendly warning Moriah had responded, with a groan, and in a voice that was almost sepulchral in its awful solemnity, *"When I mo'n I mo'n!"*

Perhaps an idea of the unusual presence of this great black woman may be conveyed by the fact that when she said, as she was wont to do in speaking of her own name, *"* I'm named Moriah —after a Bible mountain," there seemed a sort of fitness in the name and in the juxtaposition neither the sacred eminence or the woman suffered a loss of dignity.

And this woman it was who, after eight years of respectable wifehood and but four weeks of mourning her lost mate, calmly announced that she was to be married again.

The man of her choice—I use the expression advisedly—was a neighbor whom she had always known, a widower whose bereavement was of three months' longer standing than her own.

The courtship must have been brief and to the point, for it was positively known that he and his *fiancée* had met but three times in the interval when the banns were published.

He had been engaged to whitewash the kitchen

6

in which she had pursued her vocation as cook for the writer's family.

The whitewashing was done in a single morning, but a second coating was found necessary, and it is said by one of her fellow-servants, who professes to have overheard the remark, that while Pete was putting the finishing-touches to the bit of chimney back of her stove, Moriah, who stooped at the oven door beside him, basting a roast turkey, lifted up her stately head and said, archly, breaking her mourning record for the first time by a gleaming display of ivory and coral as she spoke,

"Who'd 'a' thought you'd come into my kitchen to do yo' *secon' co'tin'*, Pete?"

At which, so says our informant, the whitewash brush fell from the delighted artisan's hands, and in a shorter time than is consumed in the telling, a surprised and smiling man was sitting at her polished kitchen table chatting cosily with his mourning hostess, while she served him with giblets and gravy and rice and potatoes "an' coffee b'iled expressly."

It was discovered that the kitchen walls needed a third coating. This took an entire day, "because," so said Pete, "de third coat, hit takes mo' time to soak in."

7

And then came the announcement. Moriah herself, apparently in nowise embarrassed by its burden, bore the news to us on the following morning. There was no visible change of front in her bearing as she presented herself — no abatement of her mourning.

"Mis' Gladys," she said, simply, "I come ter give you notice dat I gwine take fo' days off, startin' nex' Sunday."

"I hope you are not in any new trouble, Moriah?" I said, sympathetically.

"Well, I don' know ef I is or not. Me an' Pete Pointdexter, we done talked it over, an' we come ter de conclusion ter marry."

I turned and looked at the woman—at her black garments, her still serious expression. Surely my hearing was playing me false. But catching my unspoken protest, she had already begun to explain.

"Dey ain't no onrespec' ter de dead, Mis' Gladys, in *marryin'*," she began. "De onrespec' is in de *carryin's on* folks does *when* dey marry. Pete an' me, we 'low ter have eve'ything quiet an' solemncholy—an' pay all due respects—right an' left. Of co'se Pete's chillen stands up fur dey mammy, an' dey don't take no stock in him ma'yin' ag'in. But Ca'line she

8

"A SURPRISED AND SMILING MAN WAS SITTING AT HER POLISHED KITCHEN TABLE" been dead *long enough*—mos' six mont's—countin' fo' weeks ter de mont'. An' as fur me, I done 'ranged ter have eve'ything did ter show respec's ter Numa." (Numa was her deceased husband.) "De organ-player he gwine march us in chu'ch by de same march he played fur Numa's fun'al, an' look like dat in itse'f is enough ter show de world dat I ain't forgot Numa. An', tell de trufe, Mis' Gladys, ef Numa was ter rise up f'om his grave, I'd sen' Pete a-flyin' so fast you could sen' eggs ter market on his coat tail.

"You see, de trouble is I done had my eye on Pete's chillen ever sence dey mammy died, an' ef dey ever was a set o' onery, low-down, sassy, no-'count little niggers dat need takin' in hand by a able-bodied step-mammy, dey a-waitin' fur me right yonder in Pete's cabin. My hand has des nachelly itched to take aholt o' dat crowd many a day—an' ever sence I buried Numa of co'se I see de way was open. An' des as soon as I felt like I could bring myse'f to it, I—well— Dey warn't no use losin' time, an' so *I tol' you, missy, dat de kitchen need' white-washin'.*"

"And so you sent for him—and proposed to him, did you?"

"P'opose to who, Mis' Gladys? I'd see Pete in de sinkin' swamp 'fo' I'd p'opose to him!"

"Then how did you manage it, pray?"

"G'way, Mis' Gladys! Any wide-awake widder 'oman dat kin get a widder man whar he
can't he'p but see her move round at her work
for two days hand-runnin', an' can't mesmerize
him so's he'll ax her to marry him— Um—hm!
I'd ondertake ter do dat, even ef I warn't no
cook; but wid seasonin's an' flavors to he'p me—
Law, chile! dey warn't no yearthly 'scape fur
dem chillen!

"I would 'a' waited," she added, presently—
"I would 'a' waited a reas'nable time, 'cep'n dat
Pete started gwine ter chu'ch, an' you know
yo'se'f, missy, when a well-favored widder man
go ter seek consolation f'om de pulpit, he's
might' ap' ter find it in de congergation."

As I sat listening to her quiet exposition of
her scheme, it seemed monstrous.

"And so, Moriah," I spoke now with a ring
of real severity in my voice—"and so you are
going to marry a man that you confess you don't
care for, just for the sake of getting control of
his children? I wouldn't have believed it of
you."

"Well—partly, missy." She smiled a little
now for the first time. "Partly on dat account,
an' partly on his'n. Pete's wife Ca'line, she was

a good 'oman, but she was mighty puny an' peevish ; an' besides dat, she was one o' deze heah naggers, an' Pete is allus had a purty hard pull, an' I lay out ter give him a better chance. Eve'y bit o' whitewashin' he'd git ter do 'roun' town, Ca'line she'd swaller it in medicine. But she was a good 'oman, Ca'line was. Heap o' deze heah naggers is good 'omans ! Co'se I don't say I *loves* Pete, but I looks ter come roun' ter 'im in time. Ef I didn't, I wouldn't have him."

"And how about his loving you ?"

"Oh, Mis' Gladys, you is so searching !" She chuckled. "Co'se he *say* he loves me already better'n he love Ca'line, but of co'se a widder man he feels obleeged ter talk dat-a-way. An' ef he didn't have the manners ter say it, I wouldn't have him, to save his life ; but *ef he meant it, I'd despise him.* After Ca'line lovin' de groun' he tread fur nine long yeahs, he ain't got no right ter love *no* 'oman better'n he love her des 'caze he's a-projec'in' ter git married to 'er. But of co'se, Mis' Gladys, I ca'culates ter outstrip Ca'line in co'se o' time. Ef I couldn't do dat— an' she in 'er grave—*an' me a cook*—I wouldn't count myse'f much. An' den, time I outstrips her an' git him over, heart *an'* soul, I'll know it by de signs."

11

"Why will you know it more than you know it now? He can but swear it to you."

"Oh no, missy. When de rock bottom of a man's heart warms to a 'oman, he eases off f'om swearin' 'bout it. Deze heah men wha' swear so much, dey swear des as much ter convince dey-selves as dey does ter ketch a 'oman's ear. No, missy. Time I got him heart *an'* soul, I looks for him to commence to th'ow up Ca'line's ways ter me. Heap of 'em does dat des ter ease dey own consciences an' pacify a dead 'oman's ghost. Dat's de way a man nachelly do. But he won't faze me, so long as I holds de fort! An' fur de chillen, co'se quick as I gits 'em broke in I'll see dat dey won't miss Ca'line none. Dat little teether, I done tol' Pete ter fetch her over ter me right away. Time I doctors her wid proper teas, an' washes her in good warm pot-liquor, I'll make a fus'-class baby out'n her."

Moriah had always been a good woman, and as she stood before me, laying bare the scheme that, no matter what the conditions, had in it the smallest selfish consideration, I felt my heart warm to her again, and I could not but feel that the little whitewasher—a kindly, hard-pressed family man of slight account—would do well to lay his brood upon her ample bosom.

Of course *she* was marrying *him,* and her acquisition of family would inevitably become pensioners upon our bounty ; but this is not a great matter in a land where the so-called "cultivation" of the soil is mainly a question of pruning and selection, and clothes grow upon the commonest bush.

As she turned to go, I even offered her my best wishes, and when I laughingly asked her if I might help her with her wedding-dress, she turned and looked at me.

"Bless yo' heart, Mis' Gladys," she exclaimed, *"I ain't gwine out o' mo'nin'!* I gwine marry Pete in des what I got on my back. I'll *marry* him, an' I'll take dem little no-'counts o' his'n, an' I'll make *folks* out'n 'em 'fo' I gits th'ough wid 'em, ef Gord spares me; but he nee'n't ter lay out ter come in 'twix' me an' my full year o' mo'nin' fur Numa. When I walks inter dat chu'ch, 'cep'n' fur de owange wreaf, which of co'se in a Christian ma'iage I'm boun' ter wear, folks 'll be a heap mo' 'minded o' Numa 'n dey will o' de bridegroom. An' dem chillen o' his'n, which ain't nuver is had no proper mo'nin' fur dey mammy—no mo' 'n what color Gord give 'em in dey skins—I gwine put 'em in special secon' mo'nin', 'cordin' to de time dey ought ter been

13

wearin' it; an' when we walks up de island o' de chu'ch, dey got ter foller, two by two, keepin' time ter de fun'al march. You come ter de weddin', Mis' Gladys, an' I lay you'll 'low dat I done fixed it so dat, while I'm a-lookin' out fur de livin', de dead ain't gwine feel slighted, right nur left."

She was starting away again, and once more, while I wished her joy, I bade her be careful to make no mistake. A note of sympathy in my voice must have touched the woman, for she turned, and coming quite up to me, laid her hand upon my lap.

"Missy," she said, "I don't believe I gwine make no mistake. You know I allus did love chillen, an' I ain't nuver is had none o' my own, an' dis heah seemed like my chance. An' I been surveyin' de lan'scape o'er tryin' ter think about eve'ything I can do *ter start right*. I'm a-startin' wid dem chillen, puttin' 'em in mo'nin' fur Ca'line. Den, fur Pete, I gwine ring de changes on Ca'line's goodness tell he ax me, *for Gord sake, ter stop*, so, in years ter come, he won't have nothin' ter th'ow up ter me. An' you know de reason I done tooken fo' days off, missy? I gwine on a weddin'-trip down ter Pine Bluff, an' I wants time ter pick out a few little weddin'-presents to fetch home ter Pete."

"Pete!" I cried. "Pete is going with you, of course?"

"Pete gwine wid me? Who sesso? No, ma'am! Why, missy, how would it look fur me ter go a-skylarkin' roun' de country wid Pete— *an' me in mo'nin'?*

"No, indeedy! I gwine leave Pete home ter take keer dem chillen, an' I done set him a good job o' whitewashin' to do while I'm gone, too. De principles' weddin'-present I gwine fetch Pete is a fiddle. Po' Pete been wantin' a good fiddle all his life, an' he 'ain't nuver is had one. But, of co'se, I don't 'low ter let him play on it tell de full year of mo'nin' is out."

AN OPTICAL DILEMMA

AN OPTICAL DILEMMA

ELDER BRADLEY had lost his spectacles, and he was in despair. He was nearly blind without them, and there was no one at home to hunt them for him. His wife had gone out visiting for the afternoon; and he had just seen Dinah, the cook, stride gleefully out the front gate at the end of the lane, arrayed in all her "s'ciety uniform," on her way to a church funeral. She would not be home until dark.

It was growing late in the afternoon, and the elder had to make out his report to be read at the meeting of the session this evening. It *had to be done.*

He could not, from where he sat, distinguish the pink lion's head from the purple rose-buds on the handsome new American Brussels rug that his wife had bought him as a Christmas gift

—to lay under her sewing-machine—although he could put out his boot and touch it. How could he expect to find anything so small as a pair of spectacles ?

The elder was a very old man, and for years his focal point had been moving off gradually, until now his chief pleasures of sight were to be found out-of-doors, where the distant views came gratefully to meet him.

He could more easily distinguish the dark glass insulators from the little sparrows that sometimes came to visit them upon the telegraph pole a quarter of a mile away than he could discriminate between the beans and the pie that sometimes lay together on his dinner plate.

Indeed, when his glasses stayed lost over meal-times, as they had occasionally done, he had, after vainly struggling to locate the various viands upon his plate and suffering repeated palatal disappointments, generally ended by stirring them all together, with the declaration that he would at least get one certain taste, and abide by it.

This would seem to show him to have been an essentially amiable man, even though he was occasionally mastered by such outbursts of impatience as this; for, be it said to his credit, he always left a clean plate.

The truth is, Elder Bradley was an earnest, good man, and he had tried all his life, in a modest, undeclared way, to be a Christian philosopher. And he would try it now. He had been, for an hour after his mishap, walking more rapidly than was his habit up and down the entire length of the hall that divided the house into two distinct sides, and his head had hung low upon his bosom. He had been pondering. Or perhaps he had been praying. His dilemma was by no means a thing to be taken lightly.

Suddenly realizing, however, that he had squandered the greater part of a valuable afternoon in useless repining, he now lifted his head and glanced about him.

"I'm a-goin' to find them blame spec's—eyes or no eyes!" He spoke with a steady voice that had in it the ring of the invincible spirit that dares failure. And now, having resolved and spoken, he turned and entered the dining-room— and sat down. It was here that he remembered having last used the glasses. He would sit here and think.

It was a rather small room, which would have been an advantage in ordinary circumstances.

But to the elder its dimensions were an insur-
mountable difficulty. How can one compass a
forty-rod focus within the limits of a twelve by
sixteen foot room ?

But if his eyes could not help him, his hands
must. He had taken as few steps as possible in
going about the room, lest he should tread upon
the glasses unawares ; and now, stepping ginger-
ly, and sometimes merely pushing his feet along,
he approached his writing-table and sat down before it. Then he began to feel. It was a tedious
experiment and a hazardous one, and after a few
moments of nervous and fruitless groping, he
sought relief in expression.

"That's right! turn over !" he exclaimed.
"I s'pose you're the red ink ! Now if I could
jest capsize the mucilage-bottle an' my bag o'
snuff, an' stir in that Seidlitz-powder I laid out
here to take, it would be purty cheerful for them
fiddle-de-dees an' furbelows thet's layin' everywhere. I hope they'll ketch it ef anything does !
They's nothin' I feel so much like doin' ez takin'
a spoon to the whole business !"

The elder was a popular father, grandfather,
uncle, husband, and Bible-class teacher to a band
of devoted women of needle - work and hand-
painting proclivities, and his writing-table was

a favorite target for their patiently wrought love-missiles.

One of the strongest evidences of the old man's kindliness of nature was that it was only when he was wrought up to the point of desperation, as now, that he spoke his mind about the gew-gaws which his soul despised.

There are very few good old elders in the Presbyterian Church who care to have pink bows tied on their penholders, or to be reminded at every turn that they are hand-painted and daisy-decked "Dear Grandfathers." It is rather inconvenient to have to dodge a daisy or a motto every time one wants to dry a letter on his blot-ting-pad, and the hand-painted paper-cutter was never meant to cut anything.

"Yes," the good old man repeated, "ef I knowed I could stir in every blame thing thet's got a ribbon bow or a bo'quet on it, I'd take a spoon to this table now—an' stir the whole busi-ness up—an' start fresh!"

Still, as his hand tipped a bottle presently, he caught it and set it cautiously back in its place.

He had begun now to systematically feel over the table, proceeding regularly with both hands from left to right and back again, until on a last return trip he discerned the edge of the mahogany next his body. And then he said—and he said it with spirit:

"Dod blast it! They ain't here—nowheres!"

He sat still now for a moment in thought. And then he began to remember that he had sat talking to his wife at the sewing-machine just before she left the house. He rose and examined the table of the machine and the floor beneath it. Then he tried the sideboard and the window-sill, where he had read his morning chapter from St. Paul's Epistle to the Romans, chapter viii.

He even shook out the leaves of his Testament upon the floor between his knees and felt for them there. There had been a Biblical surrender of this sort more than once in the past, and he never failed to go to the Good Book for relief, even when, as now, he distinctly remembered having worn the glasses after his daily reading.

Failing to find them here, he suddenly ran his hand over his forehead with an eager movement. Many a time these very spectacles had come back to him there, and, strange to say, it was always one of the last places he remembered to examine. But they were not there now.

He chuckled, even in his despair, as he dropped his hand.

24

"I'll look there ag'in after a while. Maybe when he's afeerd I'll clair lose my soul, he'll fetch 'em back to me!"

The old man had often playfully asserted that his "guardeen angel" found his lost glasses, and laid them back on his head for him when he saw him tried beyond his strength. And maybe he was right. Who can tell? That there is some sort of so-called "supernatural" intervention in such matters there seems to be little doubt.

There is a race—of brownies, probably, or maybe they are imps—whose business in life seems to be to catch up any needed trifle—a suddenly dropped needle, the very leaf in the morning paper that the reader held a moment ago and that holds "continuations," the scissors just now at his elbow, his collar button—and to hide it until the loser swears his ultimate, most desperate swear!

When the profanity is satisfactory, the little fellows usually fetch back the missing article, lay it noiselessly under the swearer's nose, and vanish.

At other times, when the victim persistently declines profanity, they have been known to amiably restore the articles after a reasonable time, and to lay them so absurdly in evidence

25

that the hitherto forbearing man breaks his record in a volley of imprecations.

When this happens, if one has presence of mind to listen, he can distinctly hear a fine metallic titter along the tops of the furniture and a hasty scamper, as of tiny scurrying feet.

This may sound jocund, but the writer testifies that it is true.

Of course when the victim is a lady the pixies do not require of them men's oaths. But they will have only her best.

When the elder had tried in vain all the probable places where the glasses might be hidden, he began to realize that there was only one thing left for him to do. He must feel all over the floor.

He was a fat old man and short of neck.

For five years he had realized a feeling of thankfulness that the Presbyterian form of worship permitted standing in prayer. It hurt him to kneel. But nothing could hurt him so much as to fail to hand in his report to-night. Indeed, the missionary collection would be affected by it. It *must be written*.

He found a corner in the room and got down on his marrow-bones, throwing his hands forward and bringing them back in far-reaching curves, as one swimming. This was hard work, and before many minutes great drops of perspiration were falling upon the carpet and the old man's breath came in quick gasps.

"Ef I jest had the blame things *for a minute* to slip on my eyes, why, *I could find 'em*—easy enough!" he ejaculated—desperation in his voice.

And then he proceeded to say a number of things that were lacking in moderation, and consequently very sinful — in an elder of the church.

The "bad words" spoken in the vacant house fell accusingly upon the speaker's ears, and they must have startled him, for he hastened to add : "I don't see where no sense o' jestice comes in, nohow, in allowin' a man on the very eve of doin' his Christian duty to lose his most important wherewithal !"

This plea was no doubt in mild extenuation of the explosive that had preceded it, and as he turned and drew himself forward by his elbows to compass a new section of the room, which, by-the-way, seemed suddenly expanded in size, he began to realize that the plea was in itself most sinful—even more so than the outburst, perhaps, being an implication of divine injustice.

27

A lump came into his throat, and as he proceeded laboriously along on his dry swim, he felt for a moment in danger of crying.

Of course this would never do, but there was just so much emotion within him, and it had begun to ferment.

Before he realized his excitement his arms were flying about wildly and he was shrieking in a frenzy.

"But *I must have 'em! I must have 'em!* I must, I say; O Lord, I must—I MUST HAVE THEM SPECTACLES! Lor-r-d, I have work to do—FOR THEE—an' I am eager to perform it. All I ask is FIVE MINUTES' USE O' MY EYES, so thet I may pursue this search in patience—"

His voice broke in a sob.

And just now it was that his left hand, fumbling over the foot of the sewing-machine treadle, ran against a familiar bit of steel wire.

If it had connected with an ordinary electric battery, the resulting shock could scarcely have been more pronounced.

There was something really pathetic in the spasmodic grasp with which he seized the glasses, and as he rose to a sitting posture and lifted them to his eyes, his hand shook pitifully.

"Thank the Lord! *Now I can see to look for*

'em!"   And as he tremblingly brought the curved ends of the wire around his ears he exclaimed with fervor, "Yas, Lord, with Thy help I will keep my vow — an' pursue this search in patience." His wet, red face beamed with pleasure over the recovery of his near vision. So happy was he, indeed, in the new possession, that, instead of rising, he sat still in the middle of the floor, running his eyes with rapid scrutiny over the carpet near him. He sat here a long time—even forgetting his discomfort, while he turned as on a pivot as the search required. Though the missing articles did not promptly appear at his side, Bradley felt that he was having a good time, and so he was, comparatively. Of course he would find the glasses presently. He looked at his watch. What a joy to see its face! He would still have time to do the report, if he hurried a little. He began to rise by painful stages.

"Lemme see! The last thing I done was to open the sideboa'd an' cut a piece o' pie an' eat it. I *must* o' had my glasses on then. I ricollec' it was sweet-potato pie, an' it was scorched on one side. Lordy! but what a pleasure it is to look for a thing when a person *can* look!" He crossed over to the sideboard.

"Yas"—he had opened the door and was cutting another piece of pie. "Yas. Sweet-potato pie, an' burnt on one side—the side thet's left. Yas, an' I'll leave it ag'in!" He chuckled as he took a deep bite.

"Of co'se I *must* 'a' had 'em on *when I cut the pie*, or I couldn't 've *saw* it so distinc'—'an I finished that slice a-settin' down talkin' to *her* at the sewin'-machine. Ricollec' I told her how mother used to put cinnamon in hers. I'll go set there ag'in, an' maybe by lookin' 'round— They might 'a' dropped in her darnin'-basket."

It was while he sat here, running one hand through the basket and holding the slice of pie in the other, that he heard a step, and, looking up, he saw his wife standing in the door.

"Why, Ephraim! What on earth!" she exclaimed. "I lef' you there eatin' that pie fo' hours ago, an' I come back an' find you settin' there yet! You cert'n'y 'ain't forgot to make out yo' report?"

"Forgot nothin', Maria." He swallowed laboriously as he spoke. "I 'ain't done a thing sence you been gone but look for my glasses—not a blame thing. An' I'm a-lookin' for 'em yet."

Mrs. Bradley was frightened. She walked straight up to her husband and took his hand.

"Ephraim," she said, gently, and as she spoke she drew the remainder of the pie from his yielding fingers—"Ephraim, I wouldn't eat any mo' o' that heavy pie ef I was you. You ain't well. Ef you can't make no mo' headway 'n that on yo' favorite pie in fo' hours, you're shorely goin' to be took sick." She took her handkerchief and wiped his forehead. And then she added, with a sweet, wifely tenderness : "To prove to you thet you ain't well, honey, yo' glasses are on yo' nose right now. You better go lay down."

Bradley looked straight into her face for some moments, but he did not even blink. Then he said, in an awe-stricken voice : "Ef what you say is true, Maria—an' from the clairness with which I see the serious expression of yo' countenance I reckon it must be so—ef it *is* so—" He paused here, and a new light came into his eyes, and then they filled with tears. "Why, Maria honey, *of co'se it's so!* I know when I found 'em! But I was so full o' the thought thet *ef I jest had my sight* I could *look for 'em* thet I slipped 'em on my nose an' continued the search. Feel my pulse, honey ; I've no doubt you're right. I'm a-goin' to have a spell o' sickness."

"Yes, dearie, I'm 'feered you are."

The good woman drew him over to the lounge and carefully adjusted a pillow to his head. "Now take a little nap, an' I'll send word over to Elder Jones's thet you ain't feelin' well an' can't come to prayer-meetin' to-night. What you need is rest, an' a change o' subject. I jest been over to May Bennett's, an' she's give out thet she an' Pete Sanders has broke off their engagement—an' Joe Legget, why his leg's amputated clean off—an' Susan Tucker's baby had seven spasms an'—"

"That so? I'm glad to hear it, wife. But ef you send word over to him thet I ain't well, don't send tell the last minute, please. Ef you was to, he'd come by here, shore—an' they'd be questions ast, an' I couldn't stand it. Jest send word when the second bell starts a-ringin' thet I ain't well. *An' I ain't*, Maria."

"I'm convinced o' that, Ephraim—or I wouldn't send the message—an' you know it. We ain't so hard pressed for excuses thet we're goin' to lie about it. I knowed you wasn't well ez soon ez I see that piece o' pie."

Bradley coughed a little. "Appearances is sometimes deceitful, Maria. I hadn't wrastled with that pie ez unsuccessful ez I seemed. That

32

was the second slice I'd et sence you left. No, the truth is, I lost my glasses, an' I got erritated an' flew into a temper an' said things. An' the Lord, He punished me. He took my reason away. He gimme the glasses an' denied me the knowledge of 'em. But I'm thankful to Him for lettin' me have 'em—anyhow. Ef I was fo'ordained to search for 'em, it was mighty merciful in Him to loan 'em to me to do it with."

THE SECOND MRS. SLIMM

THE SECOND MRS. SLIMM

E ZRA SLIMM was a widower of nearly a year, and, as a consequence, was in a state of mind not unusual in like circumstances.

True, the said state of mind had not in his case manifested itself in the toilet bloomings, friskiness of demeanor, and protestations of youth renewed which had characterized the first signs of the same in the usual run of Simpkinsville widowers up to date. If he had for several months been mentally casting about for another wife, he had betrayed it by no outward and visible sign. The fact is Ezra's case was somewhat exceptional, as we shall presently see.

Although he was quite diminutive in size, there was in his bearing, as with hands clasped behind him he paced up and down before his lonely fireside, a distinct dignity that was not only essentially manly—it was *gentlemanly*.

The refinement of feeling underlying this no doubt aggravated the dilemma in which he found himself, and which we cannot sooner comprehend than by attending to his soliloquy as he reviewed his trials in the following somewhat rambling fashion :

"No, 'twouldn't never do in the world—never, never. 'Twouldn't never do to marry any o' these girls round here thet knows all my ups an' downs with — with pore Jinny. 'Twouldn't never do. Any girl thet knew thet her husband had been chastised by his first wife the way I've been would think thet ef she got fretted she was lettin' 'im off easy on a tongue-lashin'. An' I s'pose they is times when any woman gits sort o' wrought up, livin' day in an' day out with a man. No, 'twouldn't never do," he repeated, as, thrusting both hands in his pockets, he stopped before the fire, and steadying the top of his head against the mantel, studied the logs for a moment.

" An' so the day pore Jinny took it upon herself to lay me acrost her lap an' punish me in the presence of sech ill-mannered persons ez has seen fit to make a joke of it—though I don't see where the fun comes in—well, that day she settled the hash for number two so fur ez this town goes.

"No, 'twouldn't never do in the world! Even ef she never throwed it up to me, I'd be suspicious. She couldn't even to say clap her hands together to kill a mosquito less'n I'd think she was insinuatin'. An' jest ez quick ez any man suspicions thet his wife is a-naggin' him intentional, it's good-by happiness.

"Ef 'twasn't for that, of co'se they's more'n one young woman roun' this county thet any man might go further an' do worse than git.

"Not thet I hold it agin Jinny, now she's gone, but—"

He had resumed his promenade, extending it through a second room as he proceeded:

"—but it does seem strange how a woman gifted in prayer ez she was, an' with all her instinc's religious the way hers was, should o' been allowed to take sech satisfaction in naggin' the very one she agonized most over in prayer, which I *know* she done over me, *for I've heerd 'er.* An' ef she had o' once-t mentioned me to the Lord confidential ez a person fitten to commingle with the cherubim an' seraphim, 'stid of a pore lost sinner not fitten to bresh up their wing-feathers for 'em, I b'lieve I might o' give in. I don't wonder I 'ain't never had a call to enter the Kingdom on her ricommendation. 'Twouldn't o' been fair to the innocent angels thet would 'a' been called on to associate with me. That's the way I look at it.

"An' yit Jinny 'lowed herself thet my *out'ard ac's* was good, but bein' ez they didn't spring from a converted *heart,* they was jest nachel *hypocercy,* an' thet ef I'd o' lied an' stole, *or even answered her back,* she'd o' had more hope for me, because, sez she, a 'consistent sinner is ap' to make a consistent Christian.'

"She even tol' me one day — pore Jinny! I can see her face light up now when she said it — sez she, 'I'm ac-chilly most afeerd *to* see you converted, less'n you'll break out in some devilment you hadn't never thought about before — you're that inconsistent.'

"Sometimes I feel mean to think I don't miss 'er more'n what I do — an' she so lively, too. Tell the truth, I miss them little devils she used to print on the butter pads she set at my plate ez a warnin' to me — seem to me I miss them jest about ez much ez I miss her.

"The nearest I ever *did* come to answerin' her back — 'cept, of co'se, the time she chastised me — was the way I used regular to heat my

" 'I'M AC-CHILLY MOST AFEERD *TO* SEE YOU CONVERTED ' "

knife-blade good an' hot 'twix' two batter-cakes an' flatten that devil out *de*lib'rate. But he'd be back nex' day, pitchfork an' all.

" But with it all Jinny loved me—in her own way, of co'se. Doubt if I'll ever git another to love me ez well; 'n' don't know ez I crave it, less'n she was different dispositioned.

" I've done paid her all the respec's I know— put up a fine Bible-texted tombstone for her, an' had her daguerre'type enlarged to a po'tr'it. I don't know's I'm obligated to do any more, 'cep'n, of co'se, to wait till the year's out, which, not havin' no young children in need of a mother, I couldn't hardly do less than do."

It was about a week after this that Ezra sat beside his fire reading his paper, when his eye happened to fall upon the following paragraph among the " personals " :

"The Claybank Academy continues to thrive under the able management of Miss Myrtle Musgrove. That accomplished and popular young lady has abolished the use of the rod, and by substituting the law of kindness she has built up the most flourishing academy in the State."

Ezra read the notice three times. Then he

laid the paper down, and clapping his hand
upon it, exclaimed : "Well, I'll be doggoned
ef that ain't the woman for me! *Any* girl thet
could teach a county school an' abolish whuppin'
—not only a chance to do it, but a crowd o'
young rascals *needin'* it all around 'er, an' her
not doin' it! An' yit some other persons has
been known to strain a p'int to whup a person
they 'ain't rightly got no business *to* whup." He
read the notice again. "Purty name that, too,
Myrtle Musgrove. Sounds like a girl to go out
walkin' with under the myrtle-trees in the grove
moonlight nights, Myrtle Musgrove does.

"I declare, I ain't to say religious, but I b'lieve
that notice was sent to me providential.

"Of co'se, maybe she wouldn't look at me ef I
ast her; but one thing shore, she *can't if I
don't.*

"Claybank is a good hund'ed miles from here
'n' I couldn't leave the farm now, noways; besides, the day I start a-makin' trips from home,
talk 'll start, an' I'll be watched close-ter 'n what
I'm watched now — ef that's possible. But th'
ain't nothin' to hender me *writin'* — ez I can
see."

This idea, once in his mind, lent a new impulse to Ezra's life, a fresh spring to his gait, so

evident to solicitous eyes that during the next week even his dog noticed it and had a way of running up and sniffing about him, as if asking what had happened.

An era of hope had dawned for the hitherto downcast man simply because Miss Myrtle Musgrove, a woman he had never seen, had abolished whipping in a distant school.

Two weeks passed before Ezra saw his way clearly to write the proposed letter, but he did, nevertheless, in the interval, walk up and down his butter-bean arbor on moonlight nights, imagining Miss Myrtle beside him—Miss Myrtle, named for his favorite flower. He *had* preferred the violet, but he had changed his mind. Rose-colored crêpe-myrtles were blooming in his garden at the time. Maybe this was why he began to think of her as a pink-faced laughing girl, typified by the blushing flower. Everything was so absolutely real in her setting that the ideal girl walked, a definite embodiment of his fancy, night after night by his side, and whether it was from his life habit or an intuitive fancy, he looked *upward* into her face. He had always liked tall women.

And all this time he was trying to frame a suitable letter to the real "popular and accomplished Miss Musgrove," of Claybank Academy.

Finally, however, the ambitious and flowery document was finished.

It would be unfair to him whose postscript read, "For Your Eyes alone," to quote in full, for the vulgar gratification of prying eyes, the pathetic missive that told again the old story of a lonely home, the needed woman. But when it was sent, Ezra found the circuit of the butter-bean arbor too circumscribed a promenade, and began taking the imaginary Miss Myrtle with him down through his orchard and potato-patch.

It was during these moonlight communings that he seemed to discover that she listened while he talked — a new experience to Ezra — and that even when he expressed his awful doubts as to the existence of a personal devil she only smiled, and thought he might be right.

Oh, the joy of such companionship ! But, oh, the slowness of the mails !

A month passed, and Ezra was beginning to give up all hope of ever having an answer to his letter, when one day it came, a dainty envelope with the Claybank postmark.

Miss Musgrove thanked him for his letter.

She would see him. It would not be convenient now, but would he not come down to the academy's closing exercises in June—a month later? Until then she was very respectfully his friend, Myrtle Musgrove.

The next month was the longest in Ezra's life. Still, the Lord's calendar is faithful, and the sun not a waiter upon the moods of men.

In twenty-nine days exactly a timid little man stood with throbbing heart at the door of Claybank Academy, and in a moment more he had slipped into a back seat of the crowded room, where a young orator was ringing Poe's "Bells" through all the varying cadences of h's changing voice to a rapt audience of relations and friends. Here unobserved Ezra hoped to recover his self-possession, remove the beads of perspiration one by one from his brow with a corner of his neatly folded handkerchief, and perhaps from this vantage-ground even enjoy the delight of recognizing Miss Myrtle without an introduction.

He had barely deposited his hat beneath his chair when there burst upon his delighted vision a radiant, dark-eyed, red-haired creature in pink, sitting head and shoulders above her companions on a bench set at right angles with the audience seats, in front of the house. There were a num-

ber of women in the row, and they were without
bonnets. Evidently these were the teachers, and
of course the pink goddess was Miss Myrtle Musgrove.

Ezra never knew whether the programme was
long or short. The bells had tintinabulated
and musically welled into " Casabianca " which,
in turn, had merged into " The Queen o' the
May," and presently before he realized it Free-
dom was ringing in the closing notes of "Amer-
ica," and everybody was standing up, pupils fil-
ing out, guests shaking hands, babel reigning,
and he had seen only a single, towering, handsome woman in all the assembly.

Indeed, it had never occurred to him to doubt
his own intuition, until suddenly he heard his
own name quite near, and turning quickly, he saw
a stout matronly woman of forty years or there-
abouts standing beside him, extending her hand.

Every unmarried woman is a " young lady " by
courtesy south of Mason and Dixon's line.

"I knew you as soon as I saw you, Mr.
Slimm," she was saying. "I am Miss Musgrove. But you didn't know me," she added,
archly, while Ezra made his bravest effort at
cordiality, seizing her hand in an agony which
it is better not to attempt to describe.

Miss Musgrove's face was wholesome, and so kindly that not even a cross-eye had power to spoil it. But Ezra saw only the plain middle-aged woman—the contrast to the blooming divinity whose image yet filled his soul. And he was committed to her who held his hand, unequivocally committed in writing. If he sent heavenward an agonized prayer for deliverance from a trying crisis, his petition was soon answered. And the merciful instrument was even she of the cross-eye. Before he had found need of a word of his own, she had drawn him aside, and was saying :

" You see, Mr. Slimm, the only trouble with me is that I am already married."

"Married !" gasped Ezra, trying in vain to keep the joy out of his voice. " Married, you —you don't mean—"

" Yes, married to my profession—the only husband I shall ever take. But your letter attracted me. I am a Normal School psychology student—a hard name for a well-meaning woman —and it seemed to me you were worth investigating. So I investigated. Then I knew you ought to be helped. And so I sent for you, and I am going to introduce you to three of the sweetest girls in Dixie ; and if you can't find a wife among them, then you are not so clever as I think you—that's all about it. And here comes one of them now. Kitty, step here a minute, please. Miss Deems, my friend, Mr. Slimm."

And Miss Myrtle Musgrove was off across the room before Ezra's gasp had fully expanded into the smile with which he greeted Miss Kitty Deems, a buxom lass with freckles and dimples enough to hold her own anywhere.

Two other delightful young women were presented at intervals during the afternoon in about the same fashion, and but for a certain pink Juno who flitted about ever in sight, Ezra would have confessed only an embarrassment of riches.

"And how do you get on with my girls ?" was Miss Musgrove's greeting when, late in the evening, she sought Ezra for a moment's *tête-à-tête*.

He rubbed his hands together and hesitated.

"'Bout ez fine a set o' young ladies ez I ever see," he said, with real enthusiasm ; "but, tell the truth, I—but you've a'ready been so kind— but— There she is now ! That tall, light-complected one in pink—"

"Why, certainly, Mr. Slimm. If you say so, I'll introduce her. A fine, thorough-going girl, that. You know we have abolished whipping in the academy, and that girl thought one of her boys needed it, and she followed him home, and gave it to him there, and his father interfered, and—well, *she whipped him too.* Fine girl. Not afraid of anything on earth. Certainly I'll introduce you, if you say so."

She stopped and looked at Ezra kindly. And he saw that she knew all.

"Well, I ain't particular. Some other time," he began to say; then blushing scarlet, he seized her hand, and pressing it, said, fervently, " God bless you !"

The second Mrs. Slimm is a wholesome little body, with dimples and freckles, whom Ezra declares " God A'mighty couldn't o' made without thinkin' of Ezra Slimm an' his precize necessities."

No one but himself and Miss Musgrove ever knew the whole story of his wooing, nor why, when in due season a tiny dimpled Miss Slimm came into the family circle, it was by Ezra's request that she was called Myrtle.

APOLLO BELVEDERE

A CHRISTMAS EPISODE OF THE PLANTATION

APOLLO BELVEDERE

A CHRISTMAS EPISODE OF THE PLANTATION

H E was a little yellow man with a quizzical face and sloping shoulders, and when he gave his full name, with somewhat of a flourish, as if it might hold compensations for physical shortcomings, one could hardly help smiling. And yet there was a pathos in the cari-cature that dissipated the smile half - way. It never found voice in a laugh. The pathetic quality was no doubt a certain serious ingenuous-ness—a confiding look that always met your eye from the eager face of the diminutive wearer of second-hand coats and silk hats.

"Yas, I'm named 'Pollo Belvedere, an' my marster gi'e me dat intitlemint on account o' my shape," he would say, with a strut, on occa-sion, if he were bantered, for he had learned that the name held personal suggestions which it took a little bravado to confront. Evidently Apollo's master was a humorist.

Apollo had always been a house-servant, and had for several years served with satisfaction as coachman to his master's family; but after the breaking up, when the place went into other hands, he failed to find favor with the new-comers, who had an eye for conventional form, and so Apollo was under the necessity of accepting lower rank on the place as a field-hand. But he entered plantation circles with his head up. He had his house rearing, his toilets, and his education—all distinguishing possessions in his small world—and he was, in his way, quite a gentleman. Apollo could read a chapter from the Bible without stopping to spell. He seized his words with snap-shots and pronounced them with genius. Indeed, when not limited by the suggestions of print, as when on occasion he responded to an invitation to lead in public prayer, he was a builder of words of so noble and complex architecture that one hearing him was pleased to remember that the good Lord, being omniscient, must of course know all tongues, and would understand.

That the people of the plantation thought well

of Apollo will appear from the fact that he was more than once urged to enter the ministry; but this he very discreetly declined to do, and for several reasons. In the first place he didn't feel " called to preach " ; and in the second place he did feel called or impelled to play the fiddle ; and more than that, he liked to play dance music, and to have it " danced by."

As Apollo would have told you himself, the fact that he had never married was not because he couldn't get anybody to have him, but simply that he hadn't himself been suited. And, indeed, it is because of the romance of his life that Apollo comes at all into this little sketch that bears his name. Had he not been so pathetic in his serious and grotesque personality, the story would probably have borne the name of its heroine, Miss Lily Washington, of Lone Oak Plantation, and would have concerned a number of other people.

Lily was a beauty in her own right, and she was belle of the plantation. She stood five feet ten in her bare feet, and although she tipped the scales at a hundred and sixty, she was as slim and round as a reed, and it was well known that the grip of her firm fingers applied to the closed fist of any of the young fellows on the place would make him howl. She was an emotional creature, with a caustic tongue on occasion, and when it pleased her mood to look over her shoulder at one of her numerous admirers and to wither him with a look or a word, she did not hesitate to do it. For instance, when Apollo first asked her to marry him — it had been his habit to propose to her every day or so for a year or two past — she glanced at him askance from head to foot, and then she said: "Why, yas. Dat is, I s'pose, of co'se, you's de sample. I'd order a full-size by you in a minute." This was cruel, and seeing the pathetic look come into his face, she instantly repented of it, and walked home from church with him, dismissing a handsome black fellow, and saying only kind things to Apollo all the way. And while he walked beside her, he told her that, although she couldn't realize it, he was as tall as she, for his feet were not on the ground at all; which was in a manner true, for when Lily was gracious to him, he felt himself borne along on wings that the common people could not see.

Of course no one took Apollo seriously as Lily's suitor, much less the chocolate maid herself. But there were other lovers. Indeed, there were all the others, for that matter, but in point of eligibility the number to be seriously regarded was reduced to about two. These were Pete Peters, a handsome griff, with just enough Indian in his blood to give him an air of distinction, and a French-talking mulatto who had come up from New Orleans to repair the machinery in the sugar-house, and who was buying land in the vicinity, and drove his own sulky. Pete was less prosperous then he, but although he worked his land on shares, he owned two mules and a saddle-horse, and would be allowed to enter on a purchase of land whenever he should choose to do so. Although Pete and the New Orleans fellow, whose name was also Peter, but who was called Pierre, met constantly in a friendly enough way, they did not love each other. They both loved Lily too much for that. But they laughed good-naturedly together at Apollo and his "case," which they inquired after politely, as if it were a member of his family.

"Well, 'Pollo, how's yo' case on Miss Lily comin' on?" either one would say, with a wink at the other, and Apollo would artlessly report the state of the heavens with relation to his particular star, as when he once replied to this identical question,

"Well, Miss Lily was mighty obstropulous 'istiddy, but she is mo' cancelized dis mornin'."

It was Pete who had asked the question, and he laughed aloud at the answer. "Mo' cancelized dis mornin', is she?" he replied. "How you know she is?"

"'Caze she lemme tote her hoe all de way up f'om de field," answered the ingenuous Apollo.

"She did, did she? An' who was walkin' by her side all dat time, I like to know?"

Apollo winced a little at this, but he answered, bravely, "I don't kyah ef Pier was walkin' wid her; I was totin' her hoe, all de samee."

At this Pete seemed to forget all about Apollo and his case, and he remarked that he never could see what some folks saw in city niggers, nohow— and neither could Apollo. And they felt a momentary sense of nearness to each other that was not exactly a bond, but they did not talk any more as they walked along.

It is probable that the coming of the "city fellow" into her circle hastened to culmination more than one pending romance, and there were now various and sundry coldnesses existing between Lily and a number of the boys on the place, where there had recently existed only warm and hopeful friendships. The intruder, who had a way of shrugging his shoulders and declaring of almost any question, "Well, me, I dun'no'," seemed altogether *too sure* when it came to a question of Lily. At least so he appeared to her more timid rural lovers.

The Christmas - eve dance in the sugar - house had been for years an annual function on the plantation. At this, since her début, at fourteen, three Christmases before, Lily had held undisputed sway, and all former belles amiably accepted their places as lesser lights. But there had been some quarrelling and even a fight or two on Lily's account, indirectly, and the church people had declared against the ball, on the score of domestic peace on the place. They had fought dancing *per se* as long as they could, but Terpsichore finally waltzed up the church aisle, figuratively speaking, and flaunted her ruffled skirts in the very faces of elders and minister, and they had had to smile and give her a pew to keep her still. And she was in the church yet, a troublemaker sometimes, and a disturber of spiritual peace—but still there.

If they had forcibly ejected her, some of their most promising and important members would have followed. But they could preach to her, and so they did. Mayhap in time they would convert her and have her and her numerous vo-

taries for their own. As the reverend brother
thundered out his denunciations of the ungodly
goddess he cast his eyes often in the direction of
the leading dancer, and from her they would
wander to the small fiddler who sat beside the
tall hat in a back pew. But somehow neither
Lily nor Apollo seemed in the least conscious of
any personal appeal in his glance, and when
finally the question of the Christmas ball was
put to vote, they both rose and unequivocally
voted for it. So, for that matter, did so large a
majority that one of the elders got up and proposed that the church hold revival meetings, in
the hope of rousing her people to a realization of
her dangers. And then Lily whispered something
to her neighbor, a good old man of the church,
and he stood up and announced that Miss Lily
Washington proposed to have the revival *after
Christmas.* There was some laughter at this,
and the pastor very seriously objected to it as
thwarting the very object for which the meetings
would be held ; and then, seeing herself in danger of being vanquished in argument, Lily, blushing a fine copper-color in real maidenly embarrassment, rose in the presence of the congregation,
to say that when she proposed to have the revival
after Christmas, she "didn't mean no harm."

She was only thinking that "it was a heap better to repent 'n to backslide."

This brought down the house, an expression not usually employed in this connection, but which seems to force its way here as particularly fitting. As soon as he could get a hearing the reverend brother gave out a hymn, followed it with a short prayer, and dismissed the congregation. And on the Sunday following he gave notice that for several reasons it had been decided as expedient to postpone the revival meetings in the church until *after Christmas*. No doubt he had come over to Lily's way of thinking.

Lily was perfectly ravishing in her splendor at the dance. The white Swiss frock she wore was high in the neck, but her brown shoulders and arms shone through the thin fabric with fine effect. About her slim waist she tied a narrow ribbon of blue, and she carried a pink feather fan, and the wreath about her forehead was of lilies-of-the-valley. She had done a day's scouring for them, and they had come out of the summer hat of one of the white ladies on the coast. This insured their quality, and no doubt contributed somewhat to the quiet serenity with which she bore herself as, with her little head held like that of the Venus of Milo, she danced down the centre of the room, holding her flounces in either hand, and kicking the floor until she kicked both her slippers to pieces, when she finished the figure in her stocking feet.

She had a relay of slippers ready, and there was a scramble as to who should put them on ; but she settled that question by making 'Pollo rise, with his fiddle in his arms, and lend her his chair for a minute while she pulled them on herself. Then she let Pete and Pierre each have one of the discarded slippers as a trophy. Lily had always danced out several pairs of slippers at the Christmas dance, but she had never achieved her stocking feet in the first round until now, and she was in high glee over it. If she had been admired before, she was looked upon as a raving, tearing beauty to-night—and so she was. Fortunately 'Pollo had his fiddling to do, and this saved him from any conspicuous folly. But he kept his eyes on her, and when she grew too ravishingly lovely to his fond vision, and he couldn't stand it a minute longer in silence, he turned to the man next him, who played the bones, and remarked, " Ef—ef anybody but Gord A'mighty had a-made anything as purty as Miss Lily, dey'd 'a' stinted it somewhar," and, watching every turn, he lent his

bow to her varying moods while she tired out
one dancer after another. It was the New Orleans fellow who first lost his head utterly. He
had danced with her but three times, but while
she took another's hand and whizzed through
the figures he scarcely took his eyes from her,
and when, at about midnight, he succeeded in
getting her apart for a promenade, he poured
forth his soul to her in the picturesque English
of the quadroon quarter of New Orleans. "An'
now, to proof to you my lorv, Ma'm'selle Lee-
lee"—he gesticulated vigorously as he spoke
—"I am geeving you wan beau-u-tiful Christmas present—I am goin' to geeve you—w'at you
t'ink? My borgee!" With this he turned dramatically and faced her. They were standing
now under the shed outside the door in the
moonlight, and, although they did not see him,
Apollo stood within hearing, behind a pile of
molasses - barrels, where he had come "to cool
off."

Lily had several times been "buggy - ridin'"
with Pierre in this same "borgee," and it was
a very magnificent affair in her eyes. When
he told her that it was to be hers she gasped.
Such presents were unknown on the plantation. But Lily was a "mannerly" member of

good society, if her circle was small, and she
was not to be taken aback by any compliment
a man should pay her. She simply fanned herself, a little flurriedly, perhaps, with her feather
fan, as she said : "You sho' must be jokin',
Mr. Pier. You cert'n'y must." But Mr. Pierre
was not joking. He was never more in earnest
in his life, and he told her so, and there is no
telling what else he would have told her but
for the fact that Mr. Pete Peters happened to
come out to the shed to cool off about this
time, and as he almost brushed her shoulder,
it was as little as Lily could do to address a remark to him, and then, of course, he stopped
and chatted a while ; and after what appeared
a reasonable interval, long enough for it not to
seem that she was too much elated over it, she
remarked, "An' by-de-way, Mr. Peters, I must
tell you what a lovely Christmas gif' I have
just received by de hand of Mr. Pier. He has
jest presented me wid his yaller-wheeled buggy,
an' I sho' is proud of it." Then, turning to
Pierre, she added, "You sho' is a mighty generous gen'leman, Mr. Pier—you cert'n'y is."

Peters gave Lily one startled look, but he
instantly realized, from her ingenuous manner, that there was nothing back of the gift

of the buggy—that is, it had been, so far as she was concerned, simply a Christmas present. Pierre had not offered himself with the gift. And if this were so, well, he reckoned he could match him.

He reached forward and took Lily's fan from her hand. He hastened to do this to keep Pierre from taking it. Then, while he fanned her, he said, "Is dat so, Miss Lily, dat Mr. Pier is give you a buggy? Dat sholy is a fine Christmas gif'—it sho' is. An' sence you fin' yo'se'f possessed of a buggy, I trust you will allow me de pleasure of presentin' you wid a horse to drive *in* de buggy." He made a graceful bow as he spoke, a bow that would have done credit to the man from New Orleans. It was so well done, indeed, that Lily unconsciously bowed in return, as she said, with a look that savored a little of roguishness: "Oh, hursh, Mr. Peters! You des a-guyin' me—dat what you doin'."

"Guyin' nothin'," said Peters, grinning broadly as he noted the expression of Pierre's face. "Ef you'll jes do me de honor to accep' of my horse, Miss Lily, I'll be de proudest gen'leman on dis plantation."

At this she chuckled, and took her fan in her own hand. And then she turned to Pierre.

E 65

"You sho' has set de style o' mighty expensive Christmas gif's on dis plantation, Mr. Pier—you cert'n'y has. An' I wants to thank you bofe mos' kindly—I cert'n'y does."

Having heard this much, 'Pollo thought it time to come from his hiding, and he strolled leisurely out in the other direction first, but soon returned this way. And then he stopped, and reaching over, took the feather fan — and for a few moments he had his innings. Then some one else came along and the conversation became impersonal, and one by one they all dropped off—all except 'Pollo. When the rest had gone he and Lily found seats on the cane-carrier, and they talked a while, and when a little later supper was announced, it was the proud fiddler who took her in, while Pierre and Peters stood off and politely glared at each other; and after a while Pierre must have said something, for Peters suddenly sprang at him and tumbled him out the door and rolled him over in the dirt, and they had to be separated. But presently they laughed and shook hands, and Pierre offered Pete a cigarette, and Pete took it, and gave Pierre a light—and it was all over.

It was next day—Christmas morning—and the

young people were standing about in groups under the China-trees in the campus, when Apollo
joined them, looking unusually chipper and
beaming. He was dressed in his best—Prince
Albert, beaver, and all — and he sported a
bright silk handkerchief tied loosely about his
neck.

He was altogether a delightful figure, absolutely content with himself, and apparently at
peace with the world. No sooner had he joined
the crowd than the fellows began chaffing him,
as usual, and presently some one mentioned
Lily's name and spoke of her presents. The
two men who had broken the record for generosity in the history of plantation lovers were
looked upon as nabobs by those of lesser means.
Of course everybody knew the city fellow had
started it, and they were glad Peters had come
to time and saved the dignity of the place ; indeed he was about the only one on the plantation
who could have done it.

As they stood talking it over the two heroes
had nothing to say, of course, and 'Pollo began
rolling a cigarette—an art he had learned from
the man from New Orleans.

Finally he remarked, "Yas, Miss Lily got
sev'al mighty nice presents last night."

At this Pierre turned, laughing, and said, "I s'pose you geeve 'er somet'ing too, eh?"

"Pity you hadn't a-give her dat silk hankcher. Hit 'd become her a heap better'n it becomes you," Peters said, laughing.

"Yas, I reckon it would," said 'Pollo; "but de fact is *she* gi' *me* dis hankcher—an' of co'se I accepted it."

"But why ain't you tellin' us what you give her?" insisted Peters.

'Pollo put the cigarette to his lips, deliberately lit it, puffed several times, and then, removing it in a leisurely way, he drawled:

"Well, de fact is I heerd Mr. Pier here give her a buggy, an'—an' Mr. Peters, he up an' handed over a horse,—an' so, quick as I got a chance, I des balanced my ekalub'ium an' went an' set down beside her an' ast her ef she wouldn't do me de honor to accep' of a *driver,* an'—an' *she say yas.*

"You know I'm a coachman by trade.

"An' dat's huccome I come to say she got sev'al presents las' night."

And he took another puff of his cigarette.

NEAREST OF KIN

(ON THE PLANTATION)

NEAREST OF KIN

WHEN Tamar the laundress was married to the coachman Pompey, there was a big time on the plantation. Tamar wore white tarlatan and an orange wreath—although it was her severalth marriage—and she had six bridemaids and a train-bearer. The last, a slim little black girl of about ten years, was dressed somewhat after the fashion of the ballet, in green tarlatan with spangles, and her slender legs were carefully wrapped with gilt paper that glistened through the clocked stockings with fine effect. Otherwise the "clockings" in the black stocki-net would have lost their value.

Pompey, as groom, was resplendent in the full glare of a white duck suit, and he wore a rosette of satin ribbon—" so's to 'stinguish him out f'om de groomsmen," each of whom was likewise "ducked" out in immaculate linen; and if there were some suggestive misfits among them, there were ample laundry compensations in the way of starch and polish—a proud achievement of the bride.

There was a good deal of marching up and down the aisles of the church by the entire party before the ceremony, which was, altogether, really very effective. Pompey was as black as his bride, and his face was as carefully oiled and polished for the occasion as hers, which is saying a good deal, both as to color and shine.

After the ceremony everybody repaired, for a supper and dance, to the sugar-house, where there was a bride's cake, with all the usual accessories, such as the ring and thimble, to be cut for. And of course, before the end of the evening, there was the usual distribution of bits of cake to be "dreamed on." This last, indeed, was so important that nearly every girl on the plantation slept in a neighbor's cabin that night, so as to command the full potency of the charm by dreaming her great dream in a strange bed. The whole wedding was, in fact, so disturbing a social function that everything on the place was more or less disarranged by it—even the breakfast hour at the great house, which was fully three-quarters of an hour late next morning. But that was no great matter, as all the family had been witnesses to the wedding and were somewhat sleepy in consequence—and the "rising-bell" was a movable form anyway.

Perhaps if the nuptials had been less festive the demeanor of the bride immediately afterwards would not have been so conspicuous. As it was, however, when she appeared at the wash-house, ready for duty, on the second morning following, dressed in heavy mourning, and wearing, moreovor, a pseudo-sorrowful expression on her every-otherwise shining face, they wondered, and there was some nudging and whispering among the negroes. Some hastily concluded that the marriage had been rashly repudiated as a failure ; but when presently the groom strolled into the yard, smiling broadly, and when he proceeded with many a flourish to devotedly fill her wash-tubs from the well for his bride, they saw that there must be some other explanation. The importance of the central figure in so recent a pageant still surrounded her with somewhat of a glamour in the eyes of her companions, setting her apart, so that they were slow to ask her any questions.

Later in the day, though, when her mistress, happening to pass through the yard, saw the black-gowned figure bending low over the tubs, she hastened to the wash-shed.

"Why, Tamar," she exclaimed, "what on earth—"

At this Tamar raised her face and smiled faintly. Then, glancing down at her dress to indicate that she understood, she drawled, demurely:

"Ain't nothin' de matter, missy. I jes mo'nin' for Sister Sophy-Sophia."

"Sophy-Sophia! You don't mean—"

"Yas, 'm, I does. I means Pompey's las' wife, Sis' Sophy-Sophia. She didn't have no kinfolks to go in mo'nin' for her, an' time Pompey an' me got ingaged he made known his wushes to me, an' I promised him I'd put on mo'nin' for her soon as I married into de family. Co'se I couldn't do it 'fo' I was kin to her."

"Kin to her!" the mistress laughed. "Why, Tamar, what relation on earth are you to Pompey's former wife, I'd like to know?"

The black woman dropped the garment she was wringing and thought a moment.

"Well, missy," she said, presently, "looks to me like I'm a speritu'l foster-sister to her, ef I ain't no mo'—an' I done inherited all her rights

"'I PROMISED HIM I'D PUT ON MO'NIN' FOR HER, SOON AS MARRIED INTO DE FAMILY'"

an' privileges, so Pompey say—an' ef I 'ain't got a right to mo'n for her, *who is?* Dey tell me a 'oman is got a right to go in mo'nin' for her husband's kin anyway; but of co'se, come down to it, she warn't no blood-kin to Pompey, nohow. Howsomever, eve'ybody knows a widder or a widderer is intitled to wear *all de mo'nin' dey is;* an' his wife, why, she's intitled to a equal sheer in it, if she choose to seize her rights. I'd 'a' put it on befo' de weddin', 'cep'n I didn't have no title to it, an' it wouldn't 'a' been no comfort to her noways. Set down, missy." She began wiping off one of her wash-benches with her apron as she spoke. "Set down, mistus, an' lemme talk to you."

The situation was interesting, and the mistress sat down.

"You see, missy" — she had come nearer now, and assumed a confidential tone—" you see, Sister Sophy-Sophia she 'ain't nuver found rest yit, an' dat frets Pompey. Hit troubles 'im in de sperit—an' I promised him to try to pacify her."

"Pacify her! Why, Tamar! How can you pacify a person who is dead? And how do you knew that her spirit isn't at rest?"

The black woman turned and looked behind

75

her to make sure that no one should overhear. Then, lowering her voice, she whispered :

" Her grave 'ain't nuver settled yit, mistus. She been buried ever sence befo' Christmus, an' hit ain't evened down yit. An' dat's a shore sign of a onrestless sperit—yas, 'm."

Her face had grown suddenly anxious as she spoke. And presently she added :

" Of co'se, when a grave settles *too* quick, dat's a sign dey'll soon be another death, an' nobody don't crave to see a grave sink too sudden. But it 'll ease down gradual—ef de dead sleeps easy —yas, 'm. No, Sister Sophy-Sophia she 'ain't took no comfort in her grave yit. An' Pompey, right-eously speakin', ought to pacified her befo' he set out to marry ag'in. Heap o' 'omans would 'a' been afeerd to marry a man wid a unsunk grave on his hands—'feerd she'd ha'nt her. But I done had 'spe'unce, an' I'm mo' 'feerd o' live ha'nts 'n I is o' dead ones. I know Sis' Sophy-Sophia she's *layin' dar*—an' she *can't git out*. You know, she died o' de exclammatory rheuma-tism, an' some say hit was a jedgmint f'om heav-en. You know, Sis' Sophy-Sophia she was a devil for fun. She would have her joke. An' some say Gord A'mighty punished her an' turned eve'y bone in 'er body into funny-bones, jes to show her dat eve'y funny thing ain't to be laughed at. An' ef you ever got a sudden whack on de funny-bone in yo' elbow, missy, you know how she suffered when she was teched. An' she ain't at rest yit. She done proved dat. Of co'se, ef she died wid some'h'n' on 'er mind, we can't do nothin' for her; but ef she jes need soothin', I'll git her quieted down."

She leaned forward and resumed her washing —that is to say, she raised a garment from the suds and looked at it, turned it over idly in her hands several times, and dipped it languidly.

Her visitor watched her in amused silence for a while.

"And how are you going to soothe her, Tamar?" she asked, presently. "Tell me all about it."

At this the woman began wiping her hands upon her apron, and dropping into a seat between two of the tubs and resting her arms upon their rims, she faced her mistress.

"Of co'se, honey," she began, "de fust thing is to *wear mo'nin'* — an' dat ain't no special trouble to me — I got consider'ble black frocks lef' over from my widderhoods. An' in addition to dat, I gwine carry it around in my countenance—an' *ef she sees it*—an' I b'lieve de dead

77

does see—*maybe it 'll ease her mind.* Of co'se, when a pusson ain't able to sorrer in her heart, dey 'bleeged to wear it in dey face—"

There was something in her voice as she said these last words — an indescribable note that seemed to express detachment from all feeling in the matter—that made her listener turn and look narrowly into her face. Still, she was not in the least prepared for the hearty laughter that greeted her question.

"And don't you mourn for her in your heart, Tamar?" She eyed her narrowly as she put the question.

The black woman did not even attempt an answer. Nor did she apparently even try to control her mirth. But, after a while, when she had laughed until she was tired, she suddenly rose to her feet, and as she gathered up a handful of wet garments, and began rubbing them on the wash-board, she exclaimed, still chuckling :

"Lemme git to my washin', honey, befo' I disgrace my mo'nin'."

In a little while, however, she grew serious again, and although she still seemed to have trouble with her shoulders, that insisted upon expressing merriment, she said :

"I 'clare, I talks like a plumb hycoprite, missy

78

—I sho' does. But I ain't. No, 'm, I ain't. Of co'se I grieves for Sis' Sophy-Sophia. I'd grieve for any po' human dat can't find rest in 'er grave —an' I'm gwine to consolate her, good as I kin. Soon as de dark o' de moon comes, I gwine out an' set on her grave an' moan, an' ef dat don't ease her, maybe when her funer'l is preached she'll be comforted."

"And hasn't she had her funeral sermon yet, Tamar?"

"Oh no, 'm. 'Tain't time, hardly, yit. We mos' gin'ly waits two or three years after de buryin' befo' we has members' funer'ls preached. An' we don't nuver, sca'cely, have 'em under a year. You see, dey's a lot o' smarty folks dat 'ain't got nothin' better to do 'n to bring up things ag'in dead folks's cha'acter, so we waits tell dey been restin' in de groun' a year or so. Den a preacher he can expec' to preach dey funer'ls in peace. De fac' is, some o' our mos' piousest elders an' deacons is had so many widders show up at dey funer'ls dat de chu'ches is most of 'em passed a law dat dey compelled to wait a year or so an' give all dese heah p'omiscu'us widders time to marry off—an' save scandalizement. An' Pompey an' Sophy-Sophia dey didn't have no mo'n a broomstick weddin' nohow—but of co'se *dey did*

*have de broomstick. I'm a witness to dat, 'caze
dey borried my broom—yas, 'm.* Ricollec', I had
one o' dese heah green-handle sto'e brooms, an'
Pompey he come over to my cabin one mornin'
an' he say, ' Sis' Tamar,' he say, ' would you mind
loandin' Sis' Sophy-Sophia dat green-handle
straw broom dat you sweeps out de chu'ch-house
wid ?' You 'member, I was married to Wash
Williams dat time—Wash Williams wha' live
down heah at de cross-roads now. He's married
to Yaller Silvy now. You know dat red-head
freckled-face yaller gal dat use to sew for Mis'
Ann Powers—always wear a sailor hat—wid a
waist on her no thicker'n my wris'—an' a hitch
in her walk eve'y time she pass a man ? Dat's de
gal. She stole Wash f'om me—an' she's welcome
to 'im. Any 'oman is welcome to any man she
kin git f'om me. Dat's my principle. But dese
heah yaller freckle niggers 'ain't got no principle
to 'em. I done heerd dat all my life—an' Silvy
she done proved it. Time Wash an' me was married he was a man in good chu'ch standin'—a
reg'lar ordained sexton, at six dollars a month
—an' I done de sweepin' for him. Dat's huccome
I happened to have dat green-handle sto'e broom.
Dat's all I ever did git out o' his wages. Any
day you'd pass Rose-o'-Sharon Chu'ch dem days

you could see him settin' up on de steps, like a gent'eman, an' I sho' did take pride in him. An' now, dey tell me, Silvy she got him down to shirt-sleeves—splittin' rails, wid his breeches gallused up wid twine, while she sets in de cabin do' wid a pink caliker Mother Hubbard wrapper on fannin' 'erse'f. An' on Saturdays, when he draw his pay, you'll mos' gin'ally see 'em standin' together at de hat an' ribbon show-case in de sto'e—he grinnin' for all he's worth. An' my belief is he grins des to hide his mizry."

"You certainly were very good to do his sweeping for him." Tamar's graphic picture of a rather strained situation was so humorous that it was hard to take calmly. But her mistress tried to disguise her amusement so far as possible. To her surprise, the question seemed to restore the black woman to a fresh sense of her dignity in the situation.

"Cert'ny I done it," she exclaimed, dramatically. "Cert'ny. You reckon I'd live in de house wid a man dat 'd handle a broom? No, ma'am. Nex' thing I'd look for him to sew. No, ma'am. But I started a-tellin' you huccome I come to know dat Pompey an' Sis' Sophy-Sophia was legally married wid a broom. One day he come over to my cabin, jes like I

commenced tellin' you, an' he s'lute me wid,
'Good-mornin', Sis' Tamar; I come over to see
ef you won't please, ma'am, loand Sister Sophy-
Sophia Sanders dat straw broom wha' you
sweeps out de chu'ch-house wid, please, ma'am?'
An' I ricollec's de answer I made him. I
laughed, an' I say, 'Well, Pompey,' I say, 'I
don't know about loandin' out a chu'ch broom
to a sinner like you.' An' at dat he giggle,
'Well, we wants it to play preacher—an' dat
seems like a mighty suitable job for a chu'ch
broom.' An' of co'se wid dat I passed over de
broom, wid my best wushes to de bride; an'
when he fetched it back, I ricollec', he fetched
me a piece o' de weddin'-cake—but it warn't no
mo'n common one-two-three-fo'-cup-cake wid
about seventeen onfriendly reesons stirred into
it wid brown sugar. I 'clare, when I looks
back, I sho' is ashamed to know dat dey was
ever sech a po' weddin'-cake in my family—I
sho' is. Now you know, missy, of co'se, dese
heah broom - weddin's dey ain't writ down in
nuther co't-house nur chu'ch books—an' so ef
any o' dese heah smarty meddlers was to try to
bring up ole sco'es an' say dat Sister Sophy-
Sophia wasn't legally married, dey wouldn't be
no witnesses *but me an' de broom*, an' I'd have

to witness *for it,* an'—an' *I* wouldn't be no legal witness."

"Why wouldn't you be a legal witness, Tamar?"

"'*Caze I got de same man*—an' dat's de suspiciouses' thing dey kin bring up ag'ins' a witness—so dey tell me. Ef 'twarn't for dat, I'd 'a' had her fun'al preached las' month."

"But even supposing the matter had been stirred up—and you had been unable to prove that everything was as you wished—wouldn't your minister have preached a funeral sermon anyway?"

"Oh yas, 'm, cert'ny. On'y de fun'al he'd preach wouldn't help her to rest in her grave— dat's de on'ies' diffe'ence. Like as not dey'd git ole Brother Philemon Peters down f'om de bottom-lands to preach wrath — an' I wants grace preached at Sister Sophy-Sophia's fun'al, even ef I has to wait ten years for it. She died in pain, but I hope for her to rest in peace —an' not to disgrace heaven wid crutches under her wings, nuther. I know half a dozen loud-prayers, now, dat 'd be on'y too glad to 'tract attention away f'om dey own misdoin's by rakin' out scandalizemint on a dead 'oman. Dey'd 'spute de legalness of dat marriage in a minute,

jes to keep folks f'om lookin' up dey own weddin' papers—yas, 'm. But me an' de broom—
we layin' low, now, an' keepin' still, but we'll
speak when de time comes at de jedgmint day,
ef she need a witness."

"But tell me, Tamar, why didn't Pompey
take his bride to the church if they wanted a
regular wedding?"

"Dey couldn't, missy. Dey couldn't on account o' Sis' Sophy - Sophia's secon' husband,
Sam Sanders. He hadn't made no secon' ch'ice
yit—an', you know, when de fust one of a parted couple marries ag'in, dey 'bleeged to take
to de broomstick — less'n dey go whar 'tain't
known on 'em. Dat's de rule o' divo'cemint.
When Yaller Silvy married my Joe wid a broomstick, dat lef' me free for a chu'ch marriage.
An' I tell you, *I had it, too.* But ef she had
a'tempted to walk up a chu'ch aisle wid Joe—
an' me still onmarried—well, I wush dey'd 'a'
tried it! I'd 'a' been standin' befo' de pulpit
a-waitin' for 'em—an' I'd 'a' quoted some Scripture at 'em, too. But dey acted accordin' to
law. Dey married quiet, wid a broomstick, an'
de nex' Sunday walked in chu'ch together, took
de same pew, an' he turned her pages mannerly
for her—an' dat's de ladylikest behavior Silvy

ever been guilty of in her life, I reckon. She an' him can't nair one of 'em read, but dey sets still an' holds de book an' turns de pages—an Gord Hisself couldn't ax no mo' for chu'ch behavior. But lemme go on wid my washin', missy—for Gord's sake."

Laughing again now, she drew a match from the ledge of one of the rafters, struck it across the sole of her bare foot, and began to light the fire under her furnace. And as she flattened herself against the ground to blow the kindling pine, she added, between puffs, and without so much as a change of tone :

"Don't go, please, ma'am, tell I git dis charcoal lit to start dese shirts to bile. I been tryin' to fix my mouf to ax you is you got air ole crêpe veil you could gimme to wear to chu'ch nex' Sunday—please, ma'am ? I 'clare, I wonder what's de sign when you blowin' one way an' a live coal come right back at yer 'gins' de wind ?" And sitting upon the ground, she added, as she touched her finger to her tongue and rubbed a burnt spot upon her chin : "Pompey 'd be mighty proud ef I could walk in chu'ch by his side in full sisterly mo'nin' nex' Sunday for po' Sister Sophy-Sophia—yas, 'm. I hope you kin fin' me a ole crêpe veil, please, ma'am."

MORIAH'S MOURNING

Unfortunately for the full blossoming of this mourning flower of Afro-American civilization, as it is sometimes seen to bloom along the by-ways of plantation life, there was not a second-hand veil of crêpe forth-coming on this occasion. There were small compensations, however, in sundry effective accessories, such as a crêpe collar and bonnet, not to mention a funereal fan of waving black plumes, which Pompey flourished for his wife's benefit during the entire service. Certainly the "speritu'l foster-sister" of the mourning bride, if she witnessed the tribute paid her that Sunday morning in full view of the entire congregation—for the bridal pair occupied the front pew under the pulpit—would have been obdurate indeed if she had not been somewhat mollified.

Tamar consistently wore her mourning garb for some months, and, so far as is known, it made no further impression upon her companions than to cause a few smiles and exchanges of glances at first among those of lighter mind among them, some of whom were even so uncharitable as to insinuate that Sis' Tamar wasn't "half so grieved as she let on." The more serious, however, united in commending her act as "mos' Christian-like an'"

sisterly conduc'." And when, after the gentle
insistence of the long spring rains, added to the
persuasiveness of Tamar's mourning, the grave
of her solicitude sank to an easy level, bespeak-
ing peace to its occupant, Tamar suddenly burst
into full flower of flaming color, and the mourning period became a forgotten episode of the
past. Indeed, in reviewing the ways and doings
of the plantation in those days, it seems entitled
to no more prominence in the retrospect than
many another incident of equal ingenuousness
and novelty. There was the second wooing of
old Aunt Salina - Sue, for instance, and Uncle
'Riah's diseases ; but, as Another would say,
these are other stories.

Another year passed over the plantation, and
in the interval the always expected had happened to the house of Pompey the coachman.
It was a tiny girl child, black of hue as both her
doting parents, and endowed with the name of
her sire, somewhat feminized for her fitting into
the rather euphonious Pompeylou. Tamar had
lost her other children in infancy, and so the
pansy-faced little Pompeylou of her mid-life was
a great joy to her, and most of her leisure was
devoted to the making of the pink calico slips
that went to the little one's adorning.

On her first journey into the great world beyond the plantation, however, she was not arrayed
in one of these. Indeed, the long gown she wore
on this occasion was, like that of her mother,
as black as the rejuvenated band of crêpe upon
her father's stovepipe hat; for, be it known,
this interesting family of three was to form a
line of chief mourners on the front pew of Rose-
of-Sharon Church on the occasion of the preach-
ing of the funeral of the faithfully mourned and
long-lamented Sophy-Sophia, whose hour of
posthumous honor had at length arrived. The
obsequies in her memory had been fixed for an
earlier date, but in deference to the too-recent
arrival of her "nearest of kin" was then too
young to attend, they had been deferred by
Tamar's request, and it is safe to say that no
child was ever brought forward with more pride
at any family gathering than was the tiny Miss
Pompeylou when she was carried up the aisle
"to hear her step-mammy's funeral preached."

It was a great day, and the babe, who was
on her very best six-months-old behavior, listened with admirable placidity to the "sermon
of grace," on which at a future time she might,
perhaps, found a genealogy. Her only offence
against perfect church decorum was a some-

times rather explosive " Agoo !" as she tried to reach the ever-swaying black feather fan that was waved by her parents in turn for her benefit. Before the service was over, indeed, she had secured and torn the proud emblem into bits; but Tamar only smiled at its demolition by the baby fingers. It was a good omen, she said, and meant that the day of mourning was over.

THE DEACON'S MEDICINE

THE DEACON'S MEDICINE

WHEN the doctor drove by the Gregg farm about dusk, and saw old Deacon Gregg perched cross-legged upon his own gate-post, he knew that something was wrong within, and he could not resist the temptation to drive up and speak to the old man.

It was common talk in the neighborhood that when Grandmother Gregg made things too warm for him in-doors, the good man, her spouse, was wont to stroll out to the front gate and to take this exalted seat.

Indeed, it was said by a certain Mrs. Frequent, a neighbor of prying proclivities and ungentle speech, that the deacon's wife sent him there as a punishment for misdemeanors. Furthermore, this same Mrs. Frequent did even go so far as to watch for the deacon, and when she would see him laboriously rise and resignedly poise

93

himself upon the narrow area, she would remark :

" Well, I see Grandma Gregg has got the old
man punished again. Wonder what he's been up
to now ?"

Her constant repetition of the unkind charge
finally gained for it such credence that the diminutive figure upon the gate-post became an object of mingled sympathy and mirth in the popular regard.

The old doctor was the friend of a lifetime, and
he was sincerely attached to the deacon, and
when he turned his horse's head towards the gate
this evening, he felt his heart go out in sympathy to the old man in durance vile upon his lonely perch.

But he had barely started to the gate when he
heard a voice which he recognized as the deacon's, whereupon he would have hurried away
had not his horse committed him to his first impulse by unequivocally facing the gate.

" I know three's a crowd," he called out cheer-
ily as he presently drew rein, "but I ain't a-goin'
to stay; I jest— Why, where's grandma ?" he
added, abruptly, seeing the old man alone. "I'm
shore I heard—"

" You jest heerd me a-talkin' to myself, doctor—or not to myself, exactly, neither—that is to say, when you come up I was addressin' my remarks to this here pill."

"Bill? I don't see no bill." The doctor drew his buggy nearer. He was a little deaf.

"No; I said this pill, doctor. I'm a-holdin' of it here in the pa'm o' my hand, a-studyin' over it."

"What's she a-dosin' you for now, Enoch?"

The doctor always called the deacon by his first name when he approached him in sympathy. He did not know it. Neither did the deacon, but he felt the sympathy, and it unlocked the portals of his heart.

"Well"—the old man's voice softened—"she thinks I stand in need of 'em, of co'se. The fact is, that yaller-spotted steer run ag'in her clo'es-line twice-t to-day—drug the whole week's washin' onto the ground, an' then tromped 'on it. She's inside a-renchin' an' a-starchin' of 'em over now. An' right on top o' that, I come in lookin' sort o' puny an' peaked, an' I happened to choke on a muskitty jest ez I come in, an' she declared she wasn't a-goin' to have a consumpted man sick on her hands an' a clo'es-destroyin' steer at the same time. An' with that she up an' wiped her hands on her apron, an' went an' selected this here pill

95

out of a bottle of assorted sizes, an' instructed
me to take it. They never was a thing done mo'
delib'rate an' kind—never on earth. But of co'se
you an' she know how it plegs me to take physic.
You could mould out ice-cream in little pill
shapes an' it would gag me, even ef 'twas va-
nilly-flavored. An' so, when I received it, why,
I jest come out here to meditate. You can see
it from where you set, doctor. It's a purty size-
able one, and I'm mighty suspicious of it."

The doctor cleared his throat. "Yas, I can
see it, Enoch—of co'se."

"Could you jedge of it, doctor? That is, of
its capabilities, I mean?"

"Why, no, of co'se not—not less'n I'd taste it,
an' you can do that ez well ez I can. If it's quinine, it 'll be bitter ; an' ef it's soggy an'—"

"Don't explain no mo', doctor. I can't stand
it. I s'pose it's jest ez foolish to investigate the
inwardness of a pill a person is bound to take ez
it would be to try to lif' the veil of the future in
any other way. When I'm obligated to swaller
one of 'em, I jest take a swig o' good spring water and repeat a po'tion of Scripture and commit
myself unto the Lord. I always seem foreordain-
ed to choke to death, but I notice thet ef I recover from the first spell o' suffocation, I always

come through. But I 'ain't never took one yet thet I didn't in a manner prepare to die."

"Then I wouldn't take it, Enoch. Don't do it." The doctor cleared his throat again, but this time he had no trouble to keep the corners of his mouth down. His sympathy robbed him for the time of the humor in the situation. "No, I wouldn't do it—doggone ef I would."

The deacon looked into the palm of his hand and sighed. "Oh yas, I reckon I better take it," he said, mildly. "Ef I don't stand in need of it now, maybe the good Lord 'll sto'e it up in my system, some way, 'g'inst a future attackt."

"Well"—the doctor reached for his whip— "well, I wouldn't do it—*steer or no steer!*"

"Oh yas, I reckon you would, doctor, ef you had a wife ez worrited over a wash-tub ez what mine is. An' I had a extry shirt in wash this week, too. One little pill ain't much when you take in how she's been tantalized."

The doctor laughed outright.

"Tell you what to do, Enoch. Fling it away and don't let on. She don't question you, does she?"

"No, she 'ain't never to say questioned me, but— Well, I tried that once-t. Sampled a bitter white capsule she gave me, put it down for

quinine, an' flung it away. Then I chirped up
an' said I felt a heap better—and that wasn't no
lie—which I suppose was on account o' the relief
to my mind, which it always did seem to me cap-
sules was jest constructed to lodge in a person's
air-passages. Jest lookin' at a box of 'em 'll make
me low-sperited. Well, I taken notice thet she'd
look at me keen now an' ag'in, an' then look up
at the clock, an' treckly I see her fill the gon'd
dipper an' go to her medicine-cabinet, an' then
she come to me an' she says, says she, ' Open
yore mouth !' An' of co'se I opened it. You see
that first capsule, ez well ez the one she had jest
administered, was mostly morphine, which she had
give me to ward off a 'tackt o' the neuraligy she
see approachin', and here I had been tryin' to live
up to the requi'ements of quinine, an' wrastlin' se-
vere with a sleepy spell, which, ef I'd only knew
it, would o' saved me. Of co'se, after the second
dose-t, which I swallered, I jest let nature take its
co'se, an' treckly I commenced to doze off, an'
seemed like I was a feather-bed an' wife had hung
me on the fence to sun, an' I remember how she
seemed to be a-whuppin' of me, but it didn't hurt.
Of co'se nothin' couldn't hurt me an' me all be-
numbed with morphine. An' I s'pose what put
the feather-bed in my head was on account of it

"SAYS SHE, 'OPEN YORE MOUTH,' AN' OF CO'SE I OPENED IT"

bein' goose-pickin' time, an' she was werrited with
windy weather, an' she tryin' to fill the feather-
beds. No, I won't never try to deceive her ag'in.
It never has seemed to me thet she could have
the same respect for me after ketchin' me at it,
though she 'ain't never referred to it but once-t,
an' that was the time I was elected deacon, an'
even then she didn't do it outspoke. She seemed
mighty tender over it, an' didn't no mo'n re-
mind me thet a officer in a Christian church
ought to examine hisself mighty conscientious
an' be sure he was free of deceit, which, seemed
to me, showed a heap o' consideration. She
'ain't got a deceitful bone in her body, doctor."

"Why, bless her old soul, Enoch, you know
thet I think the world an' all o' Grandma Gregg!
She's the salt o' the earth—an' rock-salt at that.
She's saved too many o' my patients by her good
nursin', in spite o' my poor doctorin', for me not
to appreciate her. But that don't reconcile me
to the way she doses you for her worries."

"It took me a long time to see that myself,
doctor. But I've reasoned it out this a-way: I
s'pose when she feels her temper a-risin' she's
'feerd thet she might be so took up with her
troubles thet she'd neglect my health, an' so she
wards off any attackt thet might be comin' on. I.

taken notice that time her strawberry preserves all soured on her hands, an' she painted my face with iodine, a man did die o' the erysipelas down here at Battle Creek, an' likely ez not she'd heerd of it. Sir? No, I didn't mention it at the time for fear she'd think best to lay on another coat, an' I felt sort o' disfiggured with it. Wife ain't a scoldin' woman, I'm thankful for that. An' some o' the peppermints an' things she keeps to dole out to me when she's fretted with little things—maybe her yeast 'll refuse to rise, or a thunder-storm 'll kill a settin' of eggs—why, they're so disguised thet *'cep'n thet I know they're medicine—"*

" Well, Kitty, I reckon we better be a-goin'." The doctor tapped his horse. " Be shore to give my love to grandma, Enoch. An' ef you're bound to take that pill—of co'se I can't no mo'n speculate about it at this distance, but I'd advise you to keep clear o' sours an' acids for a day or so. Don't think, because your teeth are adjustable, thet none o' yore other functions ain't open to salivation. *Good*-night, Enoch."

" Oh, she always looks after that, doctor. She's mighty attentive, come to withholdin' harmful temptations. Good-bye, doctor. It's did me good to open my mind to you a little.

100

"Yas," he added, looking steadily into his palm as the buggy rolled away—"yas, it's did me good to talk to him ; but I ain't no more reconciled to you, you barefaced, high - foreheaded little roly-poly, you. Funny how a pill thet 'ain't got a feature on earth can look me out o' countenance the way it can, and frustrate my speech. Talk about whited sepulchures, an' ravenin' wolves ! I don't know how come I to let on thet I was feelin' puny to-night, nohow. I might 've knew—with all them clo'es bedaubled over—though I can't, ez the doctor says, see how me a-takin' a pill is goin' to help matters—but of co'se I wouldn't let on to him, an' he a bachelor."

He stopped talking and felt his wrist.

"Maybe my pulse is obstropulous, an' ought to be sedated down. Reckon I'll haf to kill that steer—or sell him, one—though I swo'e I wouldn't. But of co'se I swo'e that in a temper, an' temp'rate vows ain't never made 'cep'in' to be repented of."

Several times during the last few minutes, while the deacon spoke, there had come to him across the garden from the kitchen the unmistakable odor of fried chicken.

He had foreseen that there would be a good

101

supper to-night, and that the tiny globule within his palm would constitute for him a prohibi-
tion concerning it.

Grandmother Gregg was one of those worthy
if difficult women who never let anything inter-
fere with her duty as she saw it magnified by the
lenses of pain or temper. It usually pleased her
injured mood to make waffles on wash-day, and
the hen - house owed many renovations, with a
reckless upsetting of nests and roosts, to one of
her "splittin' headaches." She would often
wash her hair in view of impending company, although she averred that to wet her scalp never
failed to bring on the "neuraligy." And her
"neuraligy" in turn meant medicine for the
deacon.

It was probably the doctor's timely advice,
augmented, possibly, by the potencies of the
frying-pan, with a strong underlying sympathy
with the worrying woman within — it was, no
doubt, all these powers combined that suddenly
surprised the hitherto complying husband into
such unprecedented conduct that any one know-
ing him in his old character, and seeing him now,
would have thought that he had lost his mind.

With a swift and brave fling he threw the pill
far into the night. Then, in an access of energy

born of internal panic, he slid nimbly from his perch and started in a steady jog-trot into the road, wiping away the tears as he went, and stammering between sobs as he stumbled over the ruts :

" No, I won't—yas, I will, too—doggone shame, and she frettin' her life out—of co'se I will—I'll sell 'im for anything he'll fetch—an' I'll be a better man, yas, yas I will—but I won't swaller another one o' them blame—not ef I die for it."

This report, taken in long-hand by an amused listener by the road-side, is no doubt incomplete in its ejaculatory form, but it has at least the value of accuracy, so far as it goes, which may be had only from a verbatim transcript.

It was perhaps three-quarters of an hour later when Enoch entered the kitchen, wiping his face, nervous, weary, embarrassed. Supper was on the table. The blue-bordered dish, heaped with side bones and second joints done to a turn, was moved to a side station, while in its accustomed place before Enoch's plate there sat an ominous bowl of gruel. The old man did not look at the table, but he saw it all. He would have realized it with his eyes shut. Domestic history, as well as that of greater principalities and powers, often repeats itself.

Enoch's fingers trembled as he came near his wife, and standing with his back to the table, began to untie a broad flat parcel that he had brought in under his arm. She paused in one of her trips between the table and stove, and regarded him askance.

"Reckon I'll haf to light the lantern befo' I set down to eat, wife," he said, by way of introduction. "Isrul 'll be along d'rec'ly to rope that steer. I've done sold him." The good woman laid her dish upon the table and returned to the stove.

"Pity you hadn't 'a' sold 'im day befo' yesterday. I'd 'a' had a heap less pain in my shoulder-blade." She sniffed as she said it; and then she added, "That gruel ought to be e't warm."

By this time the parcel was open. There was a brief display of colored zephyrs and gleaming card-board. Then Enoch began re-wrapping them.

"Reckon you can look these over in the mornin', wife. They're jest a few new cross-stitch Bible texts, an' I knowed you liked Scripture motters. Where'll I lay 'em, wife, while I go out an' tend to lightin' that lantern? I told Isrul I'd set it in the stable door so's he could git that steer out o' the way immejate."

The proposal to lay the mottoes aside was a master-stroke.

The aggrieved wife had already begun to wipe her hands on her apron. Still, she would not seem too easily appeased.

"I do hope you 'ain't gone an' turned that whole steer into perforated paper, Enoch, even ef 'tis Bible-texted over."

Thus she guarded her dignity. But even as she spoke she took the parcel from his hands. This was encouragement enough. It presaged a thawing out. And after Enoch had gone out to light the lantern, it would have amused a sympathetic observer to watch her gradual melting as she looked over the mottoes :

"A VIRTUOUS WIFE IS FAR ABOVE RUBIES."

"A PRUDENT WIFE IS FROM THE LORD."

"BETTER A DINNER OF HERBS WHERE LOVE
IS—"

She read them over and over. Then she laid them aside and looked at Enoch's plate. Then she looked at the chicken-dish, and now at the bowl of gruel which she had carefully set on the back of the stove to keep warm.

"Don't know ez it would hurt 'im any ef I'd

thicken that gruel up into mush. He's took sech a distaste to soft food sense he's got that new set."

She rose as she spoke, poured the gruel back into the pot, sifted and mixed a spoonful of meal and stirred it in. This done, she hesitated, glanced at the pile of mottoes, and reflected. Then with a sudden resolve she seized the milk-pitcher, filled a cup from it, poured the milk into the little pot of mush, hastily whipped up two eggs with some sugar, added the mixture to the pot, returned the whole to the yellow bowl, and set it in the oven to brown.

And just then Enoch came in, and approached the water-shelf.

"Don't keer how you polish it, a brass lantern an' coal ile is like murder on a man's hands. It will out."

He was thinking of the gruel, and putting off the evil hour. It had been his intention to boldly announce that he hadn't taken his medicine, that he never would again unless he needed it, and, moreover, that he was going to eat his supper to-night, and always, as long as God should spare him, etc., etc., etc.

But he had no sooner found himself in the presence of long-confessed superior powers than he knew that he would never do any of these things.

His wife was thinking of the gruel too when she encouraged delay by remarking that he would better rest up a bit before eating.

"And I reckon you better soak yo' hands good. Take a pinch o' that bran out o' the safe to 'em," she added, "and ef that don't do, the Floridy water is in on my bureau."

When finally Enoch presented himself, ready for his fate, she was able to set the mush pudding, done to a fine brown, before him, and her tone was really tender as she said :

"This ain't very hearty ef you're hungry ; but you can eat it all. There ain't no interference in it with anything you've took."

The pudding was one of Enoch's favorite dishes, but as he broke its brown surface with his spoon he felt like a hypocrite. He took one long breath, and then he blurted :

"By-the-way, wife, this reminds me, I reckon you'll haf to fetch me another o' them pills. I dropped that one out in the grass—that is, ef you think I still stand in need of it. I feel consider'ble better'n I did when I come in this evenin'."

The good woman eyed him suspiciously a minute. Then here eyes fell upon the words "ABOVE

RUBIES " lying upon the table. Reaching over, she lifted the pudding-bowl aside, took the dish of fried chicken from its sub-station, and set it before her lord.

" Better save that pudd'n' for dessert, honey, an' help yo'self to some o' that chicken, an' take a potater an' a roll, and eat a couple o' them spring onions — they're the first we've had. Sence you're a-feelin' better, maybe it's jest ez well thet you mislaid that pill."

The wind blows sometimes from the east in Simkinsville, as elsewhere, and there are still occasional days when the deacon betakes himself to the front gate and sits like a nineteenth-century Simon Stilites on his pillar, contemplating the open palm of his own hand, while he enriches Mrs. Frequent's *répertoire* of gossip by a picturesque item.

But the reverse of the picture has much of joy in it ; for, in spite of her various tempers, Grandmother Gregg is a warm-hearted soul—and she loves her man. And he loves her.

Listen to him to-night, for instance, as, having finished his supper, he remarks :

" An' I'm a-goin' to see to it, from this on, thet you ain't fretted with things ez you've been,

ef I can help it, wife. Sometimes, the way I act,
I seem like ez ef I forgit you're all I've got—on
earth."

"Of co'se I reelize that, Enoch," she replies.
"We're each one all the other's got—an' that's
why I don't spare no pains to keep you in
health."

TWO GENTLEMEN OF LEISURE

TWO GENTLEMEN OF LEISURE

ONE could see at a glance that they were gentlemen as they strolled leisurely along, side by side, through Madison Square, on Christmas morning.

A certain subtle charm—let us call it a dignified aimlessness—hung about them like an easy garment, labelling them as mild despisers of ambitions, of goals, of destinations, of conventionalities.

The observer who passed from casual contemplation of their unkempt locks to a closer scrutiny perceived, even in passing them, that their shoes were not mates, while the distinct bagging at the knees of their trousers was somewhat too high in one case, and too low in the other, to encompass the knees within which were slowly, but surely, gaining tardy secondary recognitions at points more or less remote from the first impressions.

H   113

One pair was a trifle short in the legs, while the other—they of the too-low knee-marks—were turned up an inch or two above the shoes : a style which in itself may seem to savor of affectation, and yet, taken with the wearer on this occasion, dispelled suspicion.

It seemed rather a cold day to sit on a bench in Madison Square, and yet our two gentlemen, after making a casual tour of the walks, sat easily down ; and, indeed, though passers hurried by in heavy top-coats and furs, it seemed quite natural that these gentlemen should be seated.

One or two others, differing more or less as individuals from our friends, but evidently members of the same social caste, broadly speaking, were also sitting in the square, apparently as oblivious to the cold as they.

"The hardest thing to bear," the taller one, he of the short trousers, was saying, as he dropped his shapely wrist over the iron arm of the bench, "the hardest thing for the individual, under the present system, is the arbitrariness of the assignments of life. The chief advantage of the Bellamy scheme seems to me to be in its harmonious adjustments, so to speak. Every man does professionally what he can best do. If you and I had' been reared under that system, now—"

114

"What, think you, would Bellamy the prophet have made of you, Humphrey?"

"Well, sir, his government would have taken pains to discover and develop my tendency, my drift—"

"Ah, I see. I should judge that nature had endowed you with a fine bump of drift, Humphrey. But has it not been rather well cared for? The trouble with drifting is, so say the preachers, that it necessarily carries one downstream."

"To the sea, the limitless, the boundless, the ultimatum—however, this is irrelevant and frivolous. I am serious—and modest, I assure you—when I speak of my gifts. I have, as you know, a pronounced gift at repartee. Who knows what this might have become under proper development? But it has been systematically snubbed, misunderstood, dubbed impertinence, forsooth."

"If I remember aright, it was your gift of repartee that — wasn't it something of that sort which severed your connection with college?"

"Yes, and here I am. That's where the shoe pinches. Ha! and by way of literal illustration, speaking of the mal-adjustments of life, witness this boot."

The speaker languidly extended his right foot. "The fellow who first wore it had bunions, blast him, and I come into his bunion-bulge with a short great toe. As a result, here I am in New York in December, instead of absorbing sunshine and the odor of violets in Jackson Square in New Orleans, with picturesqueness and color all about me. No man could start South with such a boot as that.

"I do most cordially hope that the beastly vulgarian who shaped it has gone, as my friend Mantalini would express it, 'to the demnition bow-wows.' You see the beauty of the Bellamy business is that all callings are equally worthy. As a social factor I should have made a record, and would probably have gone into history as a wit."

"Condemn the history! You'd have gone into life, Humphrey. That's enough. You'd have gone into the home—into your own bed at night—into dinner in a dress-coat—into society, your element — into posterity in your brilliant progeny, paterfamilias—"

"Enough, Colonel. There are some things— even from an old comrade like yourself—"

"Beg pardon, Humphrey. No offence meant, I assure you.

"It's only when life's fires are burning pretty low that we may venture to stir the coals and knock off the ashes a little.

"For myself, I don't mind confessing, Humphrey, that there have been women— Don't start; there isn't even a Yule-log smouldering on my heart's hearth to-day. I can stir the smoking embers safely. I say there have been women—a woman I'll say, even—a nursemaid, whom I have seen in this park—a perfect Juno. She was well-born I'd swear, by her delicate ears, her instep, her curved nostrils—"

"Did you ever approach your goddess near enough to catch her curved articulation, Colonel? Or doubtless it flowed in angles, Anglo-Saxon pura."

"You are flippant, Humphrey. I say if this woman had had educational advantages and—and if my affairs had looked up a little, well—there's no telling! And yet, to tell you this to-day does not even warm my heart."

"Nor rattle a skeleton within its closet?"

"Not a rattle about me, sir, excepting the rattle of these beastly newspapers on my chest. Have a smoke, Humphrey?"

The Colonel presented a handful of half-burned cigar-stubs.

"No choice. They're all twenty-five-centers, assorted from a Waldorf lot."

"Thanks."

Humphrey took three. The Colonel, reserving one for his own use, dropped the rest into his outer pocket.

And now eleven men passed, smoking, eleven unapproachables, before one dropped a burning stump.

As Humphrey rose and strode indolently forward to secure the fragment, there was a certain courtliness about the man that even a pair of short trousers could not disguise. It was the same which constrains us to write him down Sir Humphrey.

"I never appropriate the warmth of another man's lips," said he, as, having first presented the light to his friend, he lit a fragment for himself. Then, pressing out the fire of the last acquisition, he laid it beside him to cool before adding it to his store.

"Nor I," responded the Colonel—"at least, I never did but once. I happened to be walking behind General Grant, and he dropped a smoking stub—"

"Which you took for Granted—"

"If you will, yes. It was a bit sentimental, I
118

know, but I rather enjoyed placing it warm from his lips to mine. It was to me a sort of calumet, a pipe of peace, for rebel that I was, and am, I always respected Grant. Then, too, I fancied that I might deceive the fragment into surrendering its choicest aroma to me, since I surprised it in the attitude of surrender, and I believe it did."

"Sentimental dog that you are!" said Sir Humphrey, smiling, as he inserted the remaining bit of his cigar into an amber tip and returned it to his lips.

"You have never disclosed to me, Humphrey, where you procured that piece of bric-à-brac?"

"Haven't I? That is because of my Bostonian reticence. No secret, I assure you. I found it, sir, in the lining of this coat. The fair donor of this spacious garment on one occasion, at least, gave a *tip* to a beggar unawares."

"Exceptional woman. Seems to me the exceptional beggar would have returned the article."

"Exceptional case. Didn't find the tip for a month. I was in Mobile at the time. I should have written my benefactress had stationary been available and had I known her name. When I returned to New York in the spring there was a placard on the house. Otherwise I should have restored the tip, and trusted to her courtesy for the reward of virtue."

" You have forgotten that that commodity is its own reward ?"

" Yes, and the only reward it ever gets, as a New Orleans wit once remarked. Hence, here we are. However, returning to my fair benefactress, I haven't much opinion of her. Any woman who would mend her husband's coat-sleeve with glue —look at this ! First moist spell, away it went. Worst of it was I happened to have no garment under it at the time. However, the incident secured me quite a handsome acquisition of linen. Happened to run against a clever little tub-shaped woman whose ample bosom, I take it, was ordered especially for the accommodation of assorted sympathies. She, perceiving my azure-veined elbow, invited me to the dispensing-room of the I. O. U. Society, of which she was a member, and presented me with a roll of garments, and—would you believe it ?—there wasn't a tract or leaflet in the bundle—and as to my soul, she never mentioned the abstraction to me. Now, that is what I call Christianity. However, I may come across a motto somewhere, yet. Of course, at my first opportunity, I put on those shirts

—one to wear, and the other three to carry. So I've given them only a cursory examination thus far."

"Which one do you consider yourself wearing, Humphrey, and which do you carry?"

"I wear the *outside* one, of course—and carry the others."

"Do you, indeed? Well, now, if I were in the situation, I should feel that I was wearing the one next my body—and carrying the other three."

"That's because you are an egotist and can't project yourself. I have the power the giftie gi'e me, and see myself as others see me. How's that for quick adaptation?"

"Quite like you. If the Scotch poet had not been at your elbow with his offering, no doubt you'd have originated something quite as good. So you may be at this moment absorbing condensed theology, *nolens volens*."

"For aught I know, yes, under my armpits. However, I sha'n't object, just so the dogmas don't crowd out my morals. My moral rectitude is the one inheritance I proudly retain. I've never sold myself—to anybody."

"Nor your vote?"

"Nor my vote. True, I have accepted trifling

gratuities on election occasions; but they never affected my vote. I should have voted the same way, notwithstanding."

"Well, sir, I am always persuaded to accept a bonus on such occasions for *abstaining*. I have been under pay from both parties, each suspecting me of standing with the opposition. Needless to say, I have religiously kept my contract. I never vote. It involves too much duplicity for a man of my profession."

"Not necessarily. I resided comfortably for quite a period in the basement of the dwelling of a certain political leader in this metropolis, once. He wished to have me register for his butler, but I stickled for private secretary, and private secretary I was written, sir, though I discovered later that the rogue had registered me as secretary to his coachman. However, the latter was the better man of the two—dropped his h's so fast that his master seemed to feel constrained to send everything to H— for repairs."

"What else could you expect for a man of *aspirations?*"

"By thunder, Humphrey, that's not bad. But do you see, by yon clock, that the dinner-hour approacheth?"

The Colonel took from his waistcoat-pocket two bits of paper.

"Somehow, I miss Irving to-day. There's nothing Irving enjoyed so much as a free dinner-ticket. I see the X. Y. Z.'s are to entertain us at 1 P.M., and the K. R. G.'s at 4."

Sir Humphrey produced two similar checks.

"Well, sir, were Irving here to-day I'd willingly present him with this Presbyterian chip. There are some things to which I remain sensitive, and I look this ticket in the face with misgivings. It means being elbowed by a lot of English-slaying mendicants in a motto-bedecked saloon, where every bite at the Presbyterian fowl seems a confession of faith that that particular gobbler, or hen, as the case may be, was fore-ordained, before the beginning of time, to be chewed by yourself—or eschewed, should you decline it. Somehow theology takes the zest out of the cranberries for me. However, *de gustibus*—"

"Well, sir, I am a philosopher, and so was Irving. Poor Irving! He was never quite square. It was he, you know, who perpetrated that famous roach fraud that went the rounds of the press. I've seen him do it. He would enter a restaurant, order a dinner, and, just before finishing, discover a huge roach, a Croton bug, floating in his plate. Of course the insects were his own contribution, but the fellow had a knack of introducing them. He could slip a specimen into his omelette soufflé, for instance, dexterously slicing it in half with his knife, with a pressure that left nothing to be desired. The interloper, compactly imbedded, immediately imparted such an atmosphere to his vicinity that even the cook would have sworn he was baked in. I blush to say I was Irving's guest on one such occasion."

"And Sir Roach paid for both dinners?"

"Bless you, yes. Sir Roach, F.R.S. (fried, roasted, or stewed). Indeed, his hospitality did not end here. We were pressed to call again, and begged not to mention the incident. Of course, this was in our more prosperous days, before either of us had taken on the stamp of our exclusiveness. Even Irving would hesitate to try it now, I fancy."

"Poor Irving! A good fellow, but morally insane. In Baton Rouge now, I believe?"

"Yes. He changed overcoats with a gentleman.

"I wonder how the cooking is in that State institution, Humphrey? Irving is such an epicure—"

"Oh, he's faring well enough, doubtless.
Trust those Louisianians for cookery. When
Irving is in New Orleans there are special houses
where he drops in on Fridays, just for *court-
bouillon*. I've known him to weed a bed of geraniums rather than miss it."

"Such are the vicissitudes of pedestrianism.
Well, *tempus fugit;* let us be going. We have
just an hour to reach our dining-hall. Here come
the crowd from church. The Christmas service
is very beautiful. Do you recall it, Humphrey?"

"Only in spots—like the varioloid."

They were quite in the crowd now, and so
ceased speaking, and presently the Colonel was
considerably in advance of his companion. So it
happened that he did not see Humphrey stop a
moment, put his foot on a bit of green paper,
drop his handkerchief, and in recovering it gather
the crumpled bill into it.

Thus it came about that when Sir Humphrey
overtook his friend, and, tapping him upon the
shoulder, invited him to follow him into a famous saloon, the Colonel raised his eyes in mild
surprise.

Sir Humphrey paid for the drinks with a ten-
dollar note, and then the two proceeded to the
side door of a well-known restaurant.

"Private dining-room, please," he said, and he dropped a quarter into the hands of the servant at the door as he led the way.

It was two hours later when, having cast up his account from the bill of fare, Sir Humphrey, calling for cigars, said : "Help yourself, Colonel. If my arithmetic is correct, we shall enjoy our smoke, have a half dollar for the waiter, and enter the Square with a whole cigar apiece in our breast pockets — at peace with the world, the flesh, and his Satanic majesty. Allow me to give you a light."

He handed the Colonel one of the free dinner-tickets of the X. Y. Z. Society.

"The Presbyterian blue-light I reserve for my own use. Witness it burn.

" Well, Colonel, I hope you have enjoyed your dinner?"

"Thoroughly, sir, thoroughly. This is one of the many occasions in my life, Humphrey, when I rejoice in my early good breeding. Were it not for that, I should feel constrained to inquire whom you throttled and robbed in crossing Fifth Avenue, two hours ago, during the forty seconds when my back was turned."

"And my pious rearing would compel me to answer, 'No one.'

"The wherewithal to procure this Christmas dinner dropped straight from heaven, Colonel. I saw it fall, and gratefully seized it, just in the middle of the crossing."

"Thanks. I have taken the liberty of helping myself to the rest of the matches, Humphrey."

"Quite thoughtful of you. We'll use one apiece for the other cigars. Do you know I really enjoyed the first half of that smoke. It was quite like renewing one's youth."

And so, in easy converse, they strolled slowly down Fifth Avenue.

As Sir Humphrey hesitated in his walk, evidently suffering discomfort from his right boot, he presently remarked :

"I say, Colonel, I think I'll call around to-morrow at a few of my friends' houses, and see if some benevolent housewife won't let me have a shoe for this right foot."

"Or why not try your cigar on the ebony janitor of the apartment - house across the way. He has access to the trash - boxes, and could no doubt secure you a shoe—maybe a pair."

"Thanks, Colonel, for the suggestion, but there are a few things I never do. I never fly in the face of Providence. I shall smoke that cigar intact."

And they walked on.

THE REV. JORDAN WHITE'S THREE GLANCES

THE REV. JORDAN WHITE'S THREE GLANCES

THE Reverend Jordan White, of Cold Spring Baptist Church, was so utterly destitute of color in his midnight blackness of hue as to be considered the most thoroughly "colored" person on Claybank plantation, Arkansas.

That so black a man should have borne the name of White was one of the few of such familiar misfits to which the world never becomes insensible from familiarity. From the time when Jordan, a half-naked urchin of six, tremblingly pronounced his name before the principal's desk in the summer free Claybank school to the memorable occasion of his registration as an Afro-American voter, the announcement had never failed to evoke a smile, accompanied many times by good-humored pleasantry.

"Well, sir," so he had often laughed, "I

reck'n dey must o' gimme de name o' White fur a joke. But de Jordan—I don' know, less'n dey named me Jordan 'caze ev'ybody was afeerd ter cross me."

From which it seems that the surname was not an inheritance.

In his clerical suit of black, with standing collar and shirt-front matched in fairness only by his marvellously white teeth and eyeballs, Jordan was a most interesting study in black and white.

There were no intermediate shades about him. Even his lips were black, or of so dark a purple as to fail to maintain an outline of color. They looked black, too.

Jordan was essentially ugly, too, with that peculiar genius for ugliness which must have inspired the familiar saying current among plantation folk, "He's so ugly tell he's purty."

There is a certain homeliness of person, a combined result of type and degree, which undeniably possesses a peculiar charm, fascinating the eye more than confessed beauty of a lesser degree or more conventional form.

Jordan was ugly in this fashion, and he who glanced casually upon his ebony countenance rarely failed to look again.

He was a genius, too, in more ways than one.

If nature gave him two startling eyes that moved independently of each other, Jordan made the most of the fact, as will be seen by the following confession made on the occasion of my questioning him as to the secret of his success as a preacher.

"Well, sir," he replied, "yer see, to begin wid: I got three glances, an' dat gimme three shots wid ev'y argimint.

"When I'm a preachin' I looks straight at one man an' lays his case out so clair he can't miss it, but, you see, all de time I'm a-layin' him out, my side glances is takin' in two mo'."

"But," I protested, "I should think he whom you are looking at and describing in so personal a manner would get angry, and—"

"So he would, sir, if he knowed I was lookin' at him. *But he don't know it.* You know, dat's my third glance an' hit's my secret glance. You see, if my reel glance went straight, I'd have ter do like de rest o' you preachers, look at one man while yer hittin' de man behin' 'im, an' dat's de way dey *think I is doin'*, whiles all de time I'm a watchin' 'im wriggle.

"Of cose, sometimes I uses my glances diff'ent ways. Sometimes I des lets 'em loose p'omiskyus fur a while tell ev'ybody see blue lightnin' in de air, an' de mo'ner's bench is full, an' when I see ev'ybody is ready ter run fur 'is life, of co'se I eases up an' settles down on whatever sinner seem like he's de leastest skeered tell I nails 'im fast."

He hesitated here a moment.

"De onies' trouble," he resumed, presently. "De onies' trouble wid havin' mixed glances is 'dat seem like hit confines a man ter preach wrath.

"So long as I tried preachin' Heaven, wid golden streets an' harp music, I nuver fe'ched in a soul, but 'cep'n' sech as was dis a-waitin' fur de open do' *to* come in. Dat's my onies' drawback, Brer Jones. Sometimes seem like when Heaven comes inter my heart I does crave ter preach it in a song. Of cose, I does preach Heaven yit, but I *bleege ter preach it f'om de Hell side, an' shoo 'em in!*"

There was, I thought, the suspicion of a twinkle lurking in the corners of his eyes throughout his talk, but it was too obscure for me to venture to interpret it by a responsive smile, and so the question was put with entire seriousness when I said :

"And yet, Jordan, didn't I hear something of your going to an oculist last summer ?"

"'I DES LETS 'EM LOOSE P'OMISKYUS, TELL EV'YBODY SEE BLUE LIGHTNIN''"

"Yas, sir. So I did. Dat's true." He laughed foolishly now.

"I did talk about goin' ter one o' deze heah occular-eye doctors las' summer, *and I went once-t*, but I ain't nuver tol' nobody, an' you mustn't say nothin' 'bout it, please, sir.

"But yer see, sir." He lowered his voice here to a confidential whisper. "Yer see dat was on account o' de ladies. I was a widder-man den, an', tell de trufe, my mixed glances was gettin' me in trouble. Yer know in dealin' wid de ladies, yer don' keer how many glances you got, yer wants ter use 'em *one at a time*. Why dey was a yaller lady up heah at de cross-roads wha' 'blongs ter my church who come purty nigh ter suein' me in de co't-house, all on account o' one o' my side glances, an' all de time, yer see, my *reel* glance, hit was settled on Mis' White, wha' sot in de middle pew—but in cose she warn't Mis' White den; she was de Widder Simpson."

"And so you have been recently married," I asked; "and how does your wife feel about the matter?

"Well, yer see, sir," he answered, laughing, "she can't say nothin', 'caze she's cross-eyed 'erse'f.

"An' lemme tell you some'h'n', boss." He lowered his tone again, implying a fresh burst of confidence, while his whole visage seemed twinkling with merriment.

"Lemme tell yer some'h'n', boss. You ain't a ma'ied man, is yer?"

I assured him that I was not married.

"Well, sir, I gwine gi'e you my advice. An' I'm a man o' 'spe'unce. I been ma'ied three times, an' of cose I done consider'ble co'tin' off'n an' on wid all three, not countin' sech p'omiskyus co'tin' roun' as any widder gemman is li'ble ter do, an' I gwine gi'e you some good advice.

"Ef ever you falls in love wid air cross-eyed lady, an' craves ter co't 'er, you des turn down de lamp low 'fo' yer comes ter de fatal p'int, ur else set out on de po'ch in de fainty moonlight, whar yer can't see 'er eyes, caze dey's nothin' puts a co'tin' man out, and meek 'im lose 'is pronouns wuss 'n a cross-eye. An' ef it hadn't o' been dat *I knowed what a cook she was,* tell de trufe, de Widder Simpson's cross-eye would o' discour'ged me off enti'ely.

"But now," he continued, chuckling; "but now I done got usen ter it; it's purty ter me— seem like hit's got a searchin' glance dat goes out'n its way ter fin' me."

Needless to say, I found the old man amusing, and when we parted at the cross-roads I was quite willing to promise to drop in some time to hear one of his sermons.

Although somewhat famed as a preacher, Jordan had made his record in the pulpit not so much on account of any powers of oratory, *per se*, as through a series of financial achievements.

During the two years of his ministry he had built a new church edifice, added the imposing parsonage which he occupied, and he rode about the country on his pastoral missions, mounted on a fine bay horse—all the result of "volunteer" contributions.

And Jordan stood well with his people; the most pious of his fold according him their indorsement as heartily as they who hung about the outskirts of his congregation, and who indeed were unconsciously supplying the glamour of his distinguished career; for the secret of Jordan's success lay especially in his power of collecting money from *sinners*. So it came about that, without adding a farthing to their usual donations, the saints reclined in cushioned pews and listened to the words of life from a prosperous, well-fed preacher, who was manifestly an acceptable sower of vital seed—seed which took root in brick and mortar, branched out in turret and gable, and flowered before their very eyes in crimson upholstery.

The truth was that Cold Spring was the only colored church known to its congregation that boasted anything approaching in gorgeousness its pulpit furnishings of red cotton velvet, and never a curious sinner dropped in during any of its services for a peep at its grandeur without leaving a sufficient quota of his substance to endow him with a comfortable sense of proprietorship in it all.

The man who has given a brick to the building of the walls of a sanctuary has always a feeling of interest in the edifice, whether he be of its fold or not, and if he return to it an old man, it will seem to yield him a sort of welcoming recognition. The brick he gave is somewhere doing its part in sustaining the whole, and the uncertainty of its whereabouts seems to bestow it everywhere.

I was not long in finding my way to Jordan's church. It was in summer time, and a large part of his congregation was composed of young girls and their escorts on the afternoon when I slipped into the pew near the door.

The church was crowded within, while the

138

usual contingent of idlers hung about the front door and open windows.

I searched Jordan's face for a few moments, in the hope of discovering whether he recognized me or not, but for the life of me I could not decide. If his "secret glance" ever discerned me in my shadowed corner, neither of the other two betrayed it.

I soon discovered that there was to be no sermon on this occasion, for which I was sorry, as I supposed that his most ambitious effort would naturally take shape in this form. Of this, however, I now have my doubts.

After the conventional opening of service with prayer, Scripture reading, and song, he passed with apparent naturalness to the collection, the ceremony to which everything seemed to tend.

The opening of this subject was again conventional, the only deviation from the ordinary manner of procedure being that, instead of the hat's passing round it was inverted upon the table beside the pulpit, while contributors, passing up the aisles, deposited their contributions and returned to their seats.

This in itself, it will be seen, elevated the collection somewhat in the scale of ceremonial importance.

For some time the house was quite astir with the procession which moved up one side and down the other, many singing fervently as they went, and dramatically holding their coins aloft as they swayed in step with the music, while above all rose the exhortations of the preacher which waxed in fervor as the first generous impulse began to wane.

"Drap in yo' dollar!" he was shouting. "Drap in yo' half dollar! Drap in yo' dime! Drap in yo' nickel. Drap in yo' nickel, I say, an' ef yer ain't got a nickel, come up an' let's pray fur yer!

"Ef yer ain't got a nickel," he repeated, encouraged by the titter that greeted this; "ef yer ain't got a nickel, come up an' let de whole congergation pray fur yer! We'll teck up a collection fur any man dat 'l stan' up an' confess he ain't wuth a nickel."

A half dozen grinning young fellows stepped up now with coins concealed in the palms of their hands.

"Come on! Come on, all you nickel boys! Come on.

"Ev'y nickel is a wheel ter keep salvation's train a-movin'! Come on, I say; bring yo' wheels!

"Ef you ain't got a big wheel fur de ingine fetch a little wheel fur de freight train! We needs a-plenty o' freight kyars on dis salvation train. 'Caze hit's loaded up heavy wid Bibles fur de heathen, an' brick an' lumber to buil' churches, an' medicine fur de sick, an' ole clo'es fur de po'—heap ob 'em wid de buttons cut off'n 'em, but dat ain't our fault, we bleeged ter sen' 'em on! Fetch on yo' little wheels, I say, fur de freight train."

There had been quite a respectable response to this appeal thus far, but again it spent itself and there was a lull when Jordan, folding his arms, and looking intently before him, in several directions apparently, exclaimed in a most tragic tone:

"My Gord! Is de salvation train done stallded right in front o' Claybank chu'ch, an' we can't raise wheels ter sen' it on?

"Lord have mussy, I say! I tell yer, my brers an' sisters, you's a-treatin' de kyar o' glory wuss'n you'd treat a ole cotton mule wagon! You is, fur a fac'!

"Ef air ole mule wagon ur a donkey-kyart was stallded out in de road in front o' dis chu'ch —don' keer ef it was loaded up wid pippy chickens, much less'n de Lord's own freight—

dey ain't one o' yer but 'd raise a wheel ter sen'
it on! You know yer would! An' heah de
salvation train is stuck deep in de mud, an' yer
know Arkansas mud *hit's mud;* hit ain't b'iled
custard; no, it ain't, an' hit sticks like glue!
Heah de glory kyar is stallded in dis tar-colored
Arkansas glue-mud, I say, an' I can't raise
wheels enough out'n dis congergation ter sen'
it on! An' dis is de Holy Sabbath day, too, de
day de Lord done special set apart *fur* h'istin'
a oxes out'n a ditch, es much less'n salvation's
train.

"Now, who gwine fetch in de nex' wheel, my
brothers, my sisters, my sinner-frien's? Who
gwine fetch a wheel? Dat's it! Heah come a
wheel—two wheels—three wheels; fetch one
mo'; heah, a odd wheel; de train's a-saggin'
down lop-sided fur *one mo' wheel!* Heah it come
—f'om a ole 'oman, too! Shame on you, boys,
ter let po' ole Aunt Charity Pettigrew, wha'
nussed yo' mammies, an' is half-blin' an' deef at
dat—shame on yer ter let 'er lif' dis train out'n
de mud! An' yer know she kyant heah me nuther. She des brung a wheel 'caze she felt de
yearth trimble, an' knowed de train was stallded!

"Oh, my brers, de yearth gwine trimble wuss'n
dat one o' deze days, an' look out de rocks don't

kiver you over! Don't hol' back dis train ef you
c'n he'p it on! I ain't axin' yer fur no paper
greenbacks to-day *to light de ingine fire!*

"I ain't a-beggin' yer fur no gol' an' silver
wheels fur de passenger trains for de saints, 'caze
yer know de passenger kyars wha' ride inter de
city o' de King, dey 'bleege ter have gol' and silver wheels ter match de golden streets; but, I
say, I ain't axin' yer fur no gol' an' silver wheels
to-day, nur no kindlin'! De train is all made up
an' de ingine is a steamin', an' de b'ilers is full.
I say *de b'ilers is full,* my dear frien's.

"Full o' what? Whar do dey git water ter
run dis gorspil train? Dis heah's been a mighty
dry season, an' de cotton-fiel's is a-beggin' now
fur water, an' I say *whar do de salvation train
git water fur de ingine?*

"Oh, my po' sinner-frien's, does you want me
ter tell yer?

"De cisterns long de track is bustin' full o'
water, an' *so long as a sinner got o' tear ter shed
de water ain't gwine run out!*"

"Yas, Lord!" "Glory!" "Amen!" and
"Amen!" with loud groans came from various parts of the house now, and many wheels
were added to Glory's train by the men about
the door, while Jordan continued:

"Don't be afeerd ter weep! De ingine o' Glory's kyar would o' gi'en out o' water long 'fo' now in deze heah summer dry-drouths if 'twarn't fur de tears o' sinners, an' de grief-stricken an' de heavy-hearted! I tell yer Glory's train stops ter teck in water at de mo'ner's bench eve'y day! So don't be afeerd to weep. But bring on de wheels!"

He paused here and looked searchingly about him.

There was no response. Stepping backward now and running both hands deep into his pockets, he dropped his oratorical tone, and, falling easily into the conversational, continued :

"Well, maybe you right! Maybe you right, my frien's settin' down by de do', an' my frien's leanin' 'gins' de choir banisters, an' I ain' gwine say no mo'. I was lookin' fur you ter come up wid some sort o' wheel, an' maybe a silver wheel ter match dat watch-chain hangin' out'n yo' waistcoat-pocket ; but maybe you right!

"When a man set still an' say nothin' while de voice is a callin' I reck'n he knows what he's a-doin'.

"He knows whether de wheels in his pocket is *fitt'n* fur de gorspil kyar ur not! An' I say ter you to-day dat ef dat money in yo' pocket

144

ain't *clean money*, don't you *dare* ter fetch it up heah !

"Ef you made dat money sneakin' roun' hen-rooses in de dark o' de moon—I don't say you is, but *ef* you is — you set right still in yo' seat an' don't *dare* ter offer it ter de Lord, I say !

"Ef you backed yo' wagon inter somebody else's watermillion patch by de roadside an' load-ed up on yo' way ter town 'fo' sunup—I don't say you is, mind yer, but *ef you is* — set right whar you is, an' do des like you been doin', 'caze de money you made on dat early mornin' wagon load ain't fitt'n fur wheels fur de gorspil train !

"An' deze yo'ng men at de winders, I say, ef de wheels in *yo'* pockets come f'om *matchin' nickels on de roadside, or kyard-playin', or may-be drivin' home de wrong pig.* (You nee'n't ter laugh. De feller dat spo'ts de shinies' stovepipe hat of a Sunday sometimes cuts de ears off'n de shoat he kills of a Sa'day, 'caze de ears got a tell-tale mark on 'em.) *An', I say, ef you got yo' money dat a-way,* won't you des move back from de winders, please, an' meck room fur some o' dem standin' behin' yer dat got good hones' wheels ter pass in !"

This secured the window crowds intact, and now Jordan turned to the congregation within.

"An' now, dear beloved." He lowered his voice. "For sech as I done specified, *let us pray!*"

He had raised his hands and was closing his eyes in prayer, when a man rose in the centre of the church.

"Brer Jordan," he began, laughing with embarrassment. "Ef some o' de brers ur sisters 'll change a dime fur me—"

Jordan opened his eyes and his hands fell.

"Bless de Lord!" he exclaimed, with feeling.

"Bless de Lord, one man done claired 'isse'f! Glory, I say! Come on up, Brer Smiff, 'n' I'll gi'e you yo' change!"

"Ef—Brer Smiff 'll loan *me* dat nickel?" said a timid voice near the window.

Smith hesitated, grinning broadly.

"Ef—ef I could o' spared de dime, Mr. Small, I'd a put it in myse'f, but—but—"

"*But nothin'!* Put de dime in de hat!"

The voice came from near the front now. "Put it all in de hat, Brer Smiff. You owes me a nickel an' I'll loan'd it to Mr. Small."

And so, amid much laughter, Smith reluctantly deposited his dime.

Others followed so fast that when Jordan exclaimed, "Who gwine be de nex'?" his words were almost lost in the commotion. Still his voice had its effect.

"Heah one mo'—two mo'—fo' mo'—eight mo'! Glory, I say! An' heah dey come in de winder! Oh, I'm proud ter see it, yo'ng men! I'm proud ter see it!"

Borrowing or making change was now the order of the moment, as every individual present who had not already contributed felt called upon thus to exonerate himself from so grave a charge.

Amid the fresh stir a tremulous female voice raised a hymn, another caught it up, and another—voices strong and beautiful; alto voices soft as flute notes blended with the rich bass notes and triumphant tenors that welled from the choir, and floated in from the windows, until the body of the church itself seemed almost to sway with the rhythmic movement of the stirring hymn

"Salvation's kyar is movin'."

Still, above all, Jordan's voice could be distinguished—as a fine musical instrument, and whether breaking through the tune in a volley of exhortations, or rising superior to it all in a rich tenor—his words thrown in snatches, or drawn out to suit his purpose—never once did it mar the wonderful harmony of the whole.

It was a scene one could not easily forget. The shaft of low sunlight that now filled the church, revealing a bouquet of brilliant color in gay feathers and furbelows, with a generous sprinkling of white heads, lit up a set of faces at once so serious and so happy, so utterly forgetful of life's frettings and cares, that I felt as I looked upon them, that their perfect vocal agreement was surely but a faint reflection of a sweet spiritual harmony, which even if it did not survive the moment, was worth a long journey thither, for in so hearty a confession of fellowship, in so complete a laying down of life's burdens, there is certainly rest and a renewal of strength.

Feeling this to be a good time to slip out unobserved, I noiselessly secured my hat from beneath the pew before me, but I had hardly risen when I perceived a messenger hurrying towards me from the pulpit, with a request that I should remain a moment longer, and before I could take in the situation the singing was over and Jordan was speaking.

What he said, as nearly as I can recall it, was as follows :

" Befo' I pernounces de benediction, I wants ter 'spress de thanks o' dis chu'ch ter de 'oner'ble

"SALVATION'S KYAR IS MOVIN'!"

visitor wha' set 'isse'f so modes' in de las' pew dis evenin', *an' den sen' up de bigges' conterbutiom*, fulfillin' de words o' de Scripture, which say *de las' shill be fus' an' de fus' shill be las'.*

"Brer Chesterfiel' Jones, please ter rise an' receive de thanks o' de congergation fur dat gen'rous five-dollar bill wha' you sont up by Brer Phil Dolittle."

He paused here, and feeling all eyes turned upon me, I was constrained to rise to my feet, and I think I can truly say that I have never been surprised by greater embarrassment than I felt as I hurriedly subsided to the depths of my corner. Addressing himself now to Dolittle, Jordan continued :

"I 'ain't see you walk so biggoty in a *long* time, Brer Dolittle, as you walked when you fetched up dat five dollars. Ef dis heah 'd been a cake walk yo'd o' tooken de prize, sho'.

"De nex' time dy' all gets up a cake walk on dis plantation, lemme advise you ter borry a five-dollar note *f'om somebody dat don't know yer*, ter tote when yer walk. Hit'll he'p yer ter keep yo' chin up.

"*An' dat ain't all.* Hit'll he'p *me* ter keep *my chin up* when I ca'ys dis greenback bill to de grocery to-morrer an' I'll turn it into a wheel,

too — two wheels, wid a bulge between 'em.
Now guess wha' dat is ?"

The congregation were by this time convulsed
with laughter, and some one answered aloud :

"A flour-bar'l !"

"Dat's it, Joe, a flour-bar'l ! You's a good
guesser.

"An' so now, in de name o' Col' Spring
Chu'ch, Brer Jones, I thanks you ag'in fur a
bar'l o' flour, an' I tecks it mighty kin' o' you
too, 'caze I knows deys a heap o' 'Piscopalpalian
preachers wha' *wouldn't o' done it!* Dey'd be
'feerd dat ef dey gi'e any o' de high-risin' 'Piscopalpalian flour ter de Baptists dat dey'd ruin it
wid *col' water !*"

There was so much laughter here that Jordan
had to desist for a moment, but he had not
finished.

"*But,*" he resumed, with renewed seriousness—"*But ef Christians on'y knowed it,* dey
kin put a *little leaven o' solid Christianity* in all
de charity flour dey gi'es away, an' hit'll *leaven
de whole lot* so strong dat *too much water can't
spile it,* nur *too much fire can't scorch it,* nur *too
much fore-sight* (ur whatever dis heah is de
P'esberteriums mixes in dey bread) *can't set
it so stiff it can't rise,* 'caze hit's got de strong

150

leaven o' de spirit in it, an' hit's *boun' ter come up!*

"I see de sun's gitt'n low, an' hit's time ter let down de bars an' turn de sheeps loose, an' de goats too—not sayin' deys any goats in dis flock, an' not sayin' dey ain't—but 'fo' we goes out, I wants ter say one mo' word ter Brer Do-little."

His whole face was atwinkle with merriment now.

"Dey does say, Brer Dolittle, dat riches is mighty 'ceitful an' mighty ap' ter turn a man's head, an' I tookin' notice dat arter you fetched up Brer Chesterfiel' Jones's five dollars to-day you nuver corndescended ter meck no secon' trip to de hat on Brer Dolittle's 'count.

"I did think I'd turn a searchin' glance on yer fur a minute an' shame yer up heah, but you looked so happy an' so full o' biggoty I spared yer, but yer done had time ter cool off now, an' I 'bleeged ter bring yer ter de scratch.

"Now, ef you done teched de five - dollar notch an' can't git down, we'll git somebody ter loan'd yer a greenback bill ter fetch up, an' whils' de congergation is meditatin' on dey sins I'll gi'e you back fo' dollars an' ninety-five cents."

MORIAH'S MOURNING

Amid screams of laughter poor little Dolittle,
a comical, wizen-faced old man, nervously secured a nickel from the corner of his handkerchief, and, grinning broadly, walked up with it.

"De ve'y leastest a man *kin* do," Jordan continued, as leaning forward he presented the hat
—"de ve'y *leastest* he kin do is ter *live up ter 'is
name,* an' ef my name was *Dolittle* I sho' would
try ter *live up ter dat, ef I didn't pass beyond
it!"*

And as he restored the hat to the table beside
him, he added, with a quizzical lift of his brow:

"I does try ter live up ter *my* name even, an'
yer know, my feller-sinners, hit does look like a
hard case fur a man o' my color ter live up ter
de name o' White."

He waited again for laughter to subside.

"At leas'," he resumed, seriously, "hit did
look like a hard case *at fust,* but by de grace o'
Gord I done 'skivered de way ter do it!

"Ef we all had ter live up ter our skins, hit'd
be purty hard on a heap of us; but, bless de
Lord! he don't look at de skins; he looks at de
heart!

"I tries ter keep my *heart* white, an' my *soul*
white, an' my *sperit* white! Dat's how I tries
ter live up ter *my* name wid a *white cornscience,*

bless de Lord! An' I looks fur my people ter he'p me all dey kin."

And now, amid a hearty chorus of "Amens!" and "Glorys!" he raised his hands for a benediction, which in its all-embracing scope did not fail to invoke Divine favor upon "our good 'Piscopalpalian brother, Riviren' Chesterfiel' Jones —Gord bless him."

LADY

A MONOLOGUE OF THE COW-PEN

LADY

UMH! Fur Gord sake, des look at dem cows! All squez up together 'g'ins' dem bars in dat sof' mud—des like I knowed dey gwine be—an' me late at my milkin'! You Lady! Teck yo' proud neck down f'om off dat heifer's head! Back, I tell yer! Don't tell me, Spot! Yas, I know she impose on you—yas she do. Reachin' her monst'ous mouf clair over yo' po' little muley head. Move back, I say, Lady! Ef you so biggoty, why don't you fool wid some o' dem horn cows? You is a lady, eve'y inch of yer! You knows who to fool wid. You is de uppishes' cow I ever see in all my life—puttin' on so much style—an' yo' milk so po' an' blue, I could purty nigh blue my starch clo'es wid it. Look out dar, Peggy, how you squeeze 'g'ins'

157

Lady! She ain' gwine teck none o' yo' foolish-
ness. Peggy ain't got a speck o' manners! Lady
b'longs ter de cream o' s'ciety, I have yer know,
—an' bless Gord, I b'lieve dat's all de cream dey
is about her. Hyah! fur Gord's sake lis'n at me,
passin' a joke on Lady!

I does love to pleg dem cows—dey teck it so
good-natured. Heap o' us 'omans mought teck
lessons in Christianity f'om a cow—de way she
stan' so still an' des look mild-eyed an' chaw 'er
cud when anybody sass 'er. Dey'd be a heap
less fam'ly quar'lin on dis plantation ef de 'omans
had cuds ter chaw—dat is ef dey'd be satisfied
ter chaw dey own. But ef dey was ter have 'em
'twouldn't be no time befo' dey'd be cud fights
eve'y day in de week, eve'y one thinkin' de nex'
one had a sweeter moufful 'n what she had.
Reckon we got 'nough ter go to law 'bout, wid-
out cuds—ain't we Lady? Don't start pawin' de
groun' now, des caze yer heah me speculatin' at
yo' feed - trough. I kin talk an' work too. I
ain't like you—nuver do n'air one.

I ain't gwine pay no 'tention ter none o' y'all
no mo' now tell I git yo' supper ready. Po'
little Brindle! Stan' so still, an' ain't say a
word. I'm a-fixin' yo' feed now, honey—yas, I
is! I allus mixes yo's fust, caze I know you

nuver gits in till de las' one an' some o' de rest
o' de greedies mos' gin'ally eats it up fo' you
gits it.

She's a Scriptu'al cow, Brindle is—she so
meek.

Yas, I sho' does love Brindle. Any cow dat
kin walk in so 'umble, after all de res' git done,
an' pick up a little scrap o' leavin's out'n de
trough de way she do—an' turn it eve'y bit into
good yaller butter—*dat what I calls a cow!*
Co'se I know Lady'll git in here ahead o' yer,
honey, an' eat all dis mash I'm a-mixin' so good
fur you. It do do me good to see 'er do it, too.
I sho' does love Lady—de way 'er manners sets
on 'er. She don't count much at de churn—an'
she ain't got no conscience — an' no cha'acter —
but she's a lady! Dat's huccome I puts up wid
'er. Yas, I'm a-talkin' 'bout you, Lady, an' I'm
a-lookin' at yer, too, rahin' yo' head up so cir-
cumstantial. But you meets my eye like a lady !
You ain't shame-faced, is yer ! You too well riz
—you is. *You* know dat *I* know dat yo' po'
measly sky-colored milk sours up into mighty
fine clabber ter feed yo'ng tukkeys wid—you an'
me, we knows dat, don't we ?

Hyah ! Dar, now, we done turned de joke on
all you yaller-creamers—ain't we, Lady ?

Lordy! I wonder fo' gracious ef Lady nod
her head to me accidental!

Is you 'spondin' ter me, Lady? Tell de trufe,
I spec's Lady ter twis' up 'er tongue an' talk
some day—she work 'er mouf so knowin'!

Dis heah cotton-seed ought ter be tooken out'n
her trough, by rights. Ef I could feed her on
bran an' good warm slops a while, de churn
would purty soon 'spute her rights wid de tukkeys!

A high-toned cow, proud as Lady is, ought
ter reach white-folk's table somehow-ma-ruther.
But you gits dar all the same, don't yer Lady?
You gits dar in tukkey-meat *ef dey don't reco'nize
yer!*

Well! I'm done mixin' now an' I turns my
back on de trough—an' advance ter de bars.
Lordy, how purty dem cows does look—wid dat
low sun 'g'ins' dey backs! So patient an' yit so
onpatient.

Back, now, till I teck out dese rails!

Soh, now! Easy, Spot! Easy, Lady! I does
love ter let down dese bars wid de sun in my
eyes. I loves it mos' as good as I loves ter milk.

Down she goes!

Step up quick, now, Brindle, an' git yo' place.
Lord have mussy! Des look how Brindle

meck way fur Lady! I know'd Lady'd git dar fust! I know'd it!

An' dat's huccome I mixed dat feed so purtic'lar.

I does love Lady!

A PULPIT ORATOR

A PULPIT ORATOR

OLD Reub' Tyler, pastor of Mount Zion Chapel, Sugar Hollow Plantation, was a pulpit orator of no mean parts. Though his education, acquired during his fifty-ninth, sixtieth, and sixty-first summers, had not carried him beyond the First Reader class in the local district school, it had given him a pretty thorough knowledge of the sounds of simple letter combinations. This, supplemented by a quick intuition and a correct musical ear, had aided him to really remarkable powers of interpretation, and there was now, ten years later, no chapter in the entire Bible which he hesitated to read aloud, such as contained long strings of impossible names hung upon a chain of "begats" being his favorite achievements.

A common tribute paid Reub's pulpit eloquence by reverential listeners among his flock was, " Brer Tyler is got a black face, but his speech sho' is white." The truth was that in his humble way Reub' was something of a philologist. A new word was to him a treasure, so much stock in trade, and the longer and more formidable the acquisition, the dearer its possession.

Reub's unusual vocabulary was largely the result of his intimate relations with his master, Judge Marshall, whose body-servant he had been for a number of years. The judge had long been dead now, and the plantation had descended to his son, the present incumbent.

Reub' was entirely devoted to the family of his former owners, and almost any summer evening now he might be seen sitting on the lowest of the five steps which led to the broad front veranda of the great house where Mr. John Marshall sat smoking his meerschaum. If Marshall felt amiably disposed he would often hand the old man a light, or even his own tobacco-bag, from which Reub' would fill his corn-cob pipe, and the two would sit and smoke by the hour, talking of the crops, the weather, politics, religion, anything—as the old man led the way ; for these evening communings were his affairs rather than his " Marse John's." On a recent occasion, while they sat talking in this way, Marshall was congratulating him upon his unprecedented success in conducting a certain revival then in progress, when the old man said :

"Yassir, de Lord sho' is gimme a rich harves'. But you know some'h'n', Marse John? All de power o' language th'ough an' by which I am enable ter seize on de sperit is come to me th'ough ole marster. I done tooken my pattern f'om him f'om de beginnin,' an' des de way I done heerd him argify de cases in de co't-house, dat's de way I lay out ter state my case befo' de Lord.

"I nuver is preached wid power yit on'y but 'cep' when I sees de sinner standin' 'fo' de bar o' de Lord, an' de witnesses on de stan', an' de speckletators pressin' for'ard to heah, an' de jury listenin', an *me—I'm de prosecutin' 'torney!*

"An' when I gits dat whole co't-room 'ranged 'fo' my eyes in my min', an' de pris'ner standin' in de box, I des reg'lar *lay 'im out!* You see, I knows all de law words ter do it *wid!* I des open fire on 'im, an' prove 'im a crim'nal, a law-breaker, a vagabone, a murderer in ev'y degree dey is —fus', secon', *an'* third—a reperbate, an' a blot on de face o' de yearth, tell dey ain't a chance lef' fur 'im but ter fall on 'is knees an' plead guilty !

"An' when I got 'im down, *I got 'im whar I*

want 'im, an' de work's half did. Den I shif's roun' an' ac' *pris'ner's 'torney,* an' preach grace tell I gits 'im shoutin'—des de same as ole marster use ter do—clair a man who'r or no, guilty or no guilty, step by step, nuver stop tell he'd have de last juryman blowin' 'is nose an' sniffin'—an' he'd do it wid swellin' dic'sh'nary words, too!

"Dat's de way I works it—fus' argify fur de State, den plead fur de pris'ner.

"I tell yer, Marse John," he resumed, after a thoughtful pause, "dey's one word o' ole marster's—I don'no' huccome it slipped my min', but hit was a long glorified word, an' I often wishes hit 'd come back ter me. Ef I could ricollec' dat word, hit 'd holp me powerful in my preachin'.

"Wonder ef you wouldn't call out a few dic'-sh'nary words fur me, please, sir? maybe you monght strike it."

Without a moment's reflection, Marshall, seizing at random upon the first word that presented itself, said, "How about *ratiocination?*"

The old man started as if he were shot. "Dat's hit!" he exclaimed. "Yassir, dat's hit! How in de kingdom come is you struck it de fust pop? Rasheoshinatiom! I 'clare! Dat's de ve'y word, sho's you born! Dat's what I calls a high-tone word; ain't it, now, Marse John?"

"WON'T YER PLEASE, SIR, SPELL DAT WORD OUT FER
ME SLOW?"

"Yes, Uncle Reub'; ratiocination is a good word in its place." Marshall was much amused. "I suppose you know what it means?"

"Nemmine 'bout dat," Reub' protested, grinning all over—"nemmine 'bout dat. I des gwine fetch it in when I needs a thunder-bolt! Rasheoshinatiom! Dat's a bomb-shell fur de prosecutiom! But I can't git it off now; I'm too cool. Wait tell I'm standin' in de pulpit on tip-toes, wid de sweat a-po'in' down de spine o' my back, an' fin' myse'f *des one argimint short!* Den look out fur de locomotive!

"Won't yer," he added, after a pause—"won't yer, please, sir, spell dat word out fur me slow tell I writes it down 'fo' I forgits it?"

Reaching deep into his trousers pocket, he brought forth a folded scrap of tobacco-stained paper and a bit of lead-pencil.

Notwithstanding his fondness for the old man, there was a twinkle in Marshall's eye as he began to spell for him, letter by letter, the coveted word of power.

"R," he began, glancing over the writer's shoulder.

"R," repeated Reub', laboriously writing.

"A," continued Marshall.

"R-a," repeated Reub'.

"T," said the tutor.

"R-a-t," drawled the old man, when, suddenly catching the sound of the combination, he glanced first at the letters and then with quick suspicion up into Marshall's face. The suppressed smile he detected there did its work. He felt himself betrayed.

Springing tremulously from his seat, the very embodiment of abused confidence and wrath, he exclaimed :

"Well! Hit's come ter dis, is it? One o' ole marster's chillen settin' up makin' spote o' me ter my face! I didn't spect it of yer, Marse John— I did not. It's bad enough when some o' deze heah low-down po'-white-trash town-boys hollers 'rats' at me —let alone my own white chillen what I done toted in my arms! Lemme go home an' try ter forgit dis insult ole marster's chile insulted me wid !"

It was a moment before Marshall saw where the offence lay, and then, overcome with the ludicrousness of the situation, he roared with laughter in spite of himself.

This removed him beyond the pale of forgiveness, and as Reub' hobbled off, talking to himself, Marshall felt that present protest was useless. It was perhaps an hour later when, having deposited a bag of his best tobacco in his coat pocket, and tucked a dictionary under his arm, Marshall made his way to the old man's cabin, where, after many affectionate protestations and much insistence, he finally induced him to put on his glasses and spell the word from the printed page.

He was not easily convinced. However, under the force of Marshall's kindly assurances and the testimony of his own eyes, he finally melted, and as he set back the candle and removed his glasses, he remarked, in a tone of the utmost humility,

" Well—dat's what comes o' nigger educatiom ! Des let a nigger git fur enough along ter spell out c-a-t, cat, an' r-a-t, rat, an' a few Fus' Reader varmints, an' he's ready ter conterdic' de whole dic'sh'nary.

" Des gimme dat word a few times *in my ear* good, please, sir. I wouldn't dare ter teck it in thoo my eye, 'caze don' keer what you say, when a word sets out wid r-a-t, I gwine see a open-eyed rat settin' right at de head of it blinkin' at me ev'y time I looks at it."

AN EASTER SYMBOL

A MONOLOGUE OF THE PLANTATION

AN EASTER SYMBOL

A MONOLOGUE OF THE PLANTATION

Speaker: A Black Girl.
Time: Easter Morning.

"'SCUSE me knockin' at yo' do' so early, Miss Bettie, but I'se in trouble. Don't set up in bed. Jes' lay still an' lemme talk to yer.

"I come to ax yer to please ma'am loand me a pair o' wings, mistus. No'm, I ain't crazy. I mean what I say.

"You see, to-day's Easter Sunday, Miss Bettie, an' we havin' a high time in our chu'ch. An' I'se gwine sing de special Easter carol, wid Freckled Frances an' Lame Jane jinin' in de chorus in our choir. Hit's one o' deze heah visible choirs sot up nex' to de pulpit in front o' de congergation.

"Of co'se, me singin' de high solo makes me de principlest figgur, so we 'ranged fur me to stan' in de middle, wid Frances an' Jake on my right an' lef' sides, an' I got a bran new white tarlton frock wid spangles on it, an' a Easter lily wreath all ready. Of co'se, me bein' de fust singer, dat entitles me to wear de highest plumage, an' Frances, she knows dat, an' she 'lowed to me she was gwine wear dat white nainsook lawn you gi'n 'er, an' des a plain secondary hat, an' at de p'inted time we all three got to rise an' courtesy to de congergation, an' den bu'st into song. Lame Jake gwine wear dat white duck suit o' Marse John's an' a Easter lily in his button-hole.

"Well, hit was all fixed dat-a-way, peaceable an' proper, but you know de trouble is Freckled Frances is jealous-hearted, an' she ain't got no principle. I tell you, Miss Bettie, when niggers gits white enough to freckle, you look out for 'em! Dey jes advanced fur enough along to show white ambition an' nigger principle! An' dat's a dange'ous mixture!

"An' Frances—? She ain't got no mo' principle 'n a suck-aig dorg! Ever sence we 'ranged dat Easter programme, she been studyin' up some owdacious way to outdo me to-day in de face of eve'ybody.

"But I'm jes one too many fur any yaller freckled-faced nigger. I'm black—but dey's a heap o' trouble come out o' ink bottles befo' to-day!

"I done had my eye on Frances! An' fur de las' endurin' week I taken notice ev'ry time we had a choir practisin', Frances, she'd fetch in some talk about butterflies bein' a Easter sign o' de resurrection o' de dead, an' all sech as dat. Well, I know Frances don't keer no mo' 'bout de resurrection o' de dead 'n nothin'. Frances is too tuck up wid dis life fur dat! So I watched her. An' las' night I ketched up wid 'er.

"You know dat grea' big silk paper butterfly dat you had on yo' *pi*anner lamp, Miss Bettie? She's got it pyerched up on a wire on top o' dat secondary hat, an' she's a-fixin' it to wear it to church to-day. But she don't know I know it. You see, she knows I kin sing all over her, an' dat's huccome she's a-projectin' to ketch de eyes o' de congergation!

"But ef you'll he'p me out, Miss Bettie, we'll fix 'er. You know dem yaller gauzy wings you wo'e in de tableaux? Ef you'll loand 'em to me an' help me on wid 'em terreckly when I'm dressed, I'll *be* a *whole live butterfly*, an' I bet yer when I flutters into dat choir, Freckled Frances 'll

M   177

feel like snatchin' dat lamp shade off her hat, sho's you born! An' fur once-t I'm proud I'm so black complected, caze black an' yaller, dey goes together fur butterflies !

"Frances 'lowed to kill me out to-day, but I lay when she sets eyes on de yaller-winged butterfly she'll 'preciate de resurrection o' de dead ef she never done it befo' in her life."

CHRISTMAS AT THE TRIMBLES'

CHRISTMAS AT THE TRIMBLES'

Part I

Time: Daylight, the day before Christmas.
Place: Rowton's store, Simpkinsville.

First Monologue, by Mr. Trimble:

" WHOA-A-A, there, ck, ck, ck! Back, now, Jinny! Hello, Rowton! Here we come, Jinny an' me—six miles in the slush up to the hub, an' Jinny with a unweaned colt at home. Whoa-a-a, there !

" It's good Christmus don't come but once-t a year—ain't it, Jinny ?

" Well, Rowton, you're what I call a pro-gressive business man, that's what you are. Blest ef he ain't hired a whole row o' little niggers to stand out in front of 'is sto'e an' hold horses —while he takes his customers inside to fleece 'em.

181

"Come here, Pop-Eyes, you third feller, an' ketch aholt o' Jinny's bridle. I always did like pop-eyed niggers. They look so God-forsaken an' ugly. A feller thet's afflicted with yo' style o' beauty ought to have favors showed him, an' that's why I intend for you to make the first extry to-day. The boy thet holds my horse of a Christmus Eve always earns a dollar. Don't try to open yo' eyes no wider—I mean what I say. How did Rowton manage to git you fellers up so early, I wonder. Give out thet he'd hire the first ten that come, did he? An' gives each feller his dinner an' a hat.

"I was half afeered you wouldn't be open yet, Rowton—but I was determined to git ahead o' the Christmus crowd, an' I started by starlight. I ca'culate to meet 'em all a-goin' back.

"Well, I vow, ef yo' sto'e don't look purty. Wish _she_ could see it. She'd have some idee of New York. But, of co'se, I couldn't fetch her to-day, an' me a-comin' specially to pick out her Christmus gif'. She's jest like a child. Ef she s'picions befo' hand what she's a-goin' to git, why, she don't want it.

"I notice when I set on these soap-boxes, my pockets is jest about even with yo' cash-drawer, Rowton. Well, that's what we're here for,

Fetch out all yo' purties, now, an' lay 'em along on the counter. You know *her*, an' she ain't to be fooled in quality. Reckon I *will* walk around a little an' see what you've got. I 'ain't got a idee on earth what to buy, from a broach to a barouche. Let's look over some o' yo' silver things, Rowton. Josh Porter showed me a butter-dish you sold him with a silver cow on the led of it, an' I was a-wonderin' ef, maybe, you didn't have another.

"That's it. That's a mighty fine idee, a statue like that is. It sort o' designates a thing. D'rec'-ly a person saw the cow, now, he'd s'picion the butter inside the dish. Of co'se, he'd know they wouldn't hardly be hay in it—no, ez you say, 'nor a calf.' No doubt wife 'll be a-wantin' one o' these cow-topped ones quick ez she sees Josh's wife's. She'll see the p'int in a minute —of the cow, I mean. But, of co'se, I wouldn't think o' gittin' her the same thing Josh 's got for Helen, noways. We're too near neighbors for that. Th' ain't no fun in borryin' duplicates over a stile when company drops in sudden, without a minute's warnin'.

"No, you needn't call my attention to that tiltin' ice-pitcher. I seen it soon ez I approached the case. Didn't you take notice to me a-liftin'

my hat? That was what I was a-bowin' to, that
pitcher was. No, that's the thing wife hankers
after, an' I know it, an' it's the one thing I'll
never buy her. Not thet I'd begrudge it to her—
but to tell the truth it'd pleg me to have to live
with the thing. I wouldn't mind it on Sundays
or when they was company in the house, but I
like to take off my coat, hot days, an' set around
in my shirt-sleeves, an' I doubt ef I'd have the
cheek to do it in the face of sech a thing as that.

"Fact is, when I come into a room where one
of 'em is, I sort o' look for it to tilt over of its
own accord an' bow to me an' ask me to 'be
seated.'

"You needn't to laugh. Of co'se, they's a
reason for it—but it's so. I'm jest that big of
a ninny. Ricollec' Jedge Robinson, he used to
have one of 'em—jest about the size o' this one
—two goblets an' a bowl—an' when I'd go up to
the house on a errand for pa, time pa was dis-
tric' coroner, the jedge's mother-in-law, ol' Mis'
Meredy, she'd be settin' in the back room a-
sewin,' an' when the black gal would let me in
the front door she'd sort o' whisper : 'Invite
him to walk into the parlor and be seated.' I'd
overhear her say it, an' I'd turn into the parlor, an' first thing I'd see'd be that ice-pitcher.

I don't think anybody can *set down* good, noways, when they're ast to 'be seated,' an' when, in addition to that, I'd meet the swingin' icepitcher half way to the patent rocker, I didn't have no mo' consciousness where I was a-settin' than nothin'. An' like ez not the rocker'd squawk first strain I put on it. She wasn't no mo'n a sort o' swingin' ice-pitcher herself, ol' Mis' Meredy wasn't—walkin' round the house weekdays dressed in black silk, with a lace cap on her head, an' half insultin' his company thet he'd knowed all his life. I did threaten once-t to tell her, 'No, thank you, ma'am, I don't keer to be seated—but I'll *set down* ef it's agreeable,' but when the time would come I'd turn round an' there'd be the ice-pitcher. An' after that I couldn't be expected to do nothin' but back into the parlor over the Brussels carpet an' chaw my hat-brim. But, of co'se, I was young then.

"Reckon you've heerd the tale they tell on Aleck Turnbull the day he went there in the old lady's time. She had him ast into the cushioned sanctuary — an' Aleck hadn't seen much them days — an' what did he do but gawk around an' plump hisself down into that gilt-backed rocker with a tune-playin' seat in it, an', of co'se, quick ez his weight struck it, it

185

started up a jig tune, an' they say Aleck shot
out o' that door like ez ef he'd been fired out of
a cannon. An' he never did go back to say what
he come after. I doubt ef he ever knew.

"How much did you say for the ice-pitcher,
Rowton? Thirty dollars—an' you'll let me have
it for—hush, now, don't say that. I don't see
how you could stand so close to it an' offer to
split dollars. Of co'se I ain't a-buyin' it, but
ef I was I wouldn't want no reduction on it, I'd
feel like ez ef it would always know it an' have
a sort of contemp' for me. They's suitableness
in all things. Besides, I never want no reduction on anything I buy for *her*, someways. You
can charge me reg'lar prices an' make it up on
the Christmus gif' she buys for me—that is, ef
she buys it from you. Of co'se it'll be charged.
That's a mighty purty coral broach, that grape-
bunch one, but she's so pink-complected, I don't
know ez she'd become it. I like this fish-scale
set, myself, but she might be prejerdyced ag'in'
the idee of it. You say she admired that
hand - merror, an' this pair o' side - combs—an'
she 'lowed she'd git 'em fur my Christmus gif'
ef she dared? But, of co'se, she was jokin' about
that. Poor little thing, she ain't never got over
the way folks run her about that side-saddle she

186

give me last Christmus, though I never did see anything out o' the way in it. She knew thet the greatest pleasure o' my life was in makin' her happy, and she was jest simple - hearted enough to do it—that's all—an' I can truly say thet I ain't never had mo' pleasure out of a Christmus gif' in my life than I've had out o' that side-saddle. She's been so consistent about it—never used it in her life without a-borryin' it of me, an' she does it so cunnin'. Of co'se I don't never loand it to her without a kiss. They ain't a cunnin'er play-actor on earth 'n she is, though she ain't never been to a theatre—an' wouldn't go, bein' too well raised.

"You say this pitcher wasn't there when she was here—no, for ef it had 'a' been, I know she'd 'a' took on over it. Th' ain't never been one for sale in Simpkinsville before. They've been several of 'em brought here by families besides the one old Mis' Meredy presided over—though that was one o' the first. But wife is forever a-pickin' out purty patterns of 'em in the catalogues. Ef that one hadn't 'a' give me such a setback in my early youth I'd git her this, jest to please her. Ef I was to buy this one, it an' the plush album would set each other off lovely. She's a-buyin' *it* on instalments from the same man thet en-

larged her photograph to a' ile-painted po'trait,
an' it's a dandy ! She's got me a-settin' up on
the front page, took with my first wife, which it
looks to me thet if she'd do that much to please
me, why, I might buy almost anything to please
her, don't it ? Of co'se I don't take no partic'lar
pleasure in that photograph—but she seems to
think I might, an' no doubt she's put it there to
show thet she ain't small-minded. You ricollec'
Mary Jane was plain - featured, but Kitty don't
seem to mind that ez much ez I do, now thet
she's gone an' her good deeds ain't in sight. I
never did see no use in throwin' a plain-featured
woman's looks up to her *post mortem.*

"This is a mighty purty pitcher, in my judgment, but to tell the truth I've made so much
fun o' the few swingin' pitchers thet's been in
this town that I'd be ashamed to buy it, even ef
I could git over my own obnoxion to it. But of
co'se, ez you say, everybody'd know thet I done
it jest to please her—an' I don't know thet they's
a more worthy object in a married man's life than
that.

"I s'pose I'll haf to git it for her. An' I want
a bold, outspoke dedication on it, Rowton. I ain't
a-goin' about it shamefaced. Here, gimme that
pencil. Now, I want this inscription on it, word

for word. I've got to stop over at Paul's to git him to regulate my watch, an' I'll tell him to hurry an' mark it for me, soon ez you send it over.

"Well, so long. Happy Christmus to you an' yo' folks.

"Say, Rowton, wrap up that little merror an' them side-combs au' send 'em along, too, please. So long!"

Part II

Time: Same morning.
Place: Store in Washington.

Second Monologue, by Mrs. Trimble:

"WHY, howdy, Mis' Blakes — howdy, Mis' Phemie—howdy, all. Good-mornin', Mr. Lawson. I see yo' sto'e is fillin' up early. Great minds run in the same channel, partic'larly on Christmus Eve.

"My old man started off this mornin' befo' day, an' soon ez he got out o' sight down the Simpkinsville road, I struck out for Washin'ton, an' here I am. He thinks I'm home seedin' raisins. He was out by starlight this mornin'

189

with the big wagon, an', of co'se, I know what
that means. He's gone for my Christmus gif',
an' I'm put to it to know what tremenjus thing
he's a-layin' out to fetch me—thet takes a cotton-
wagon to haul it. Of co'se I imagine everything,
from a guyaskutus down. I always did like to
git things too big to go in my stockin'. What
you say, Mis' Blakes? Do I hang up my stockin'? Well, I reckon. I hadn't quit when I got
married, an' I think that's a poor time to stop,
don't you? Partic'larly when you marry a man
twice-t yo' age, an' can't convince him thet you're
grown, noways. Yas, indeedy, that stockin' goes
up to-night—not mine, neither, but one I borry
from Aunt Jane Peters. I don't wonder y' all
laugh. Aunt Jane's foot is a yard long ef it's a'
inch, but I'll find it stuffed to-morrer mornin',
even ef the guyaskutus has to be chained to the
mantel. An' it'll take me a good hour to empty
it, for he always puts a lot o' devilment in it, an'
I give him a beatin' over the head every non-
sensical thing I find in it. We have a heap o'
fun over it, though.

"He don't seem to know I'm grown, an' I
know I don't know he's old.

"Listen to me runnin' on, an' you all nearly
done yo' shoppin'. Which do you think would

be the nicest to give him, Mr. Lawson—this silver card-basket, or that Cupid vase, or— ?

"Y'all needn't to wink. I seen you, Mis' Blakes. Ef I was to pick out a half dozen socks for him like them you're a-buyin' for Mr. Blakes, how much fun do you suppose we'd have out of it? Not much. I'd jest ez lief 'twasn't Christmus—an' so would he—though they do say his first wife give him a bolt o' domestic once-t for Christmus, an' made it up into night-shirts an' things for him du'in' the year. Think of it. No, I'm a-goin' to git him somethin' thet's got some git-up to it, an'—an' it'll be either—that—Cupid vase — or — lordy, Mr. Lawson, don't fetch out that swingin' ice-pitcher. I glimpsed it quick ez I come in the door, an', says I, 'Get thee behind me, Satan,' an' turned my back on it immejiate.

"But of co'se I ca'culated to git you to fetch it out jest for me to look at, after I'd selected his present. Ain't it a beauty? Seems to me they couldn't be a more suitable present for a man— ef he didn't hate 'em so. No, Mis' Blakes, it ain't only thet he don't never drink ice-water. I wouldn't mind a little thing like that.

"You ricollec' ol' Mis' Meredy, she used to preside over one thet they had, an' somehow he taken a distaste to her an' to ice-pitchers along

191

with her, an' he don't never lose a chance to express his disgust. When them new folks was in town last year projec'in' about the railroad, he says to me, ' I hope they won't stay, they'd never suit Simpkinsville on earth. They're the regular swingin' ice-pitcher sort. Git folks like that in town an' it wouldn't be no time befo' they'd start a-chargin' pew rent in our churches.' We was both glad when they give out thet they wasn't a-goin' to build the road. They say railroads is mighty corruptin', an' me, with my sick headaches, an' a' ingine whistle in town, no indeed! Besides, ef it was to come I know I'd be the first one run over. It's bad enough to have bulls in our fields without turnin' steam-ingines loose on us. Jest one look at them cow-ketchers is enough to frustrate a person till he'd stand stock still an' wait to be run over—jest like poor crazy Mary done down here to Cedar Springs.

"They say crazy Mary looked that headlight full in the face, jes' the same ez a bird looks at a snake, till the thing caught her, an' when the long freight train had passed over her she didn't have a single remain, not a one, though I always thought they might 've gethered up enough to give her a funeral. When I die I intend to have a funeral, even if I'm drownded at sea. They can stand on the sho'e, an' I'll be jest ez likely to know it ez them thet lay in view lookin' so ca'm. I've done give him my orders, though they ain't much danger o' me dyin' at sea, not ef we stay in Simpkinsville.

"How much are them willer rockers, Mr. Lawson? I declare that one favors my old man ez it sets there, even without him in it. Nine dollars? That's a good deal for a pants'-tearin' chair, seems to me, which them willers are, the last one of 'em, an' I'm a mighty poor hand to darn. Jest let me lay my stitches in colors, in the shape of a flower, an' I can darn ez well ez the next one, but I do despise to fill up holes jest to be a-fillin'. Yes, ez you say, them silver-mounted brier-wood pipes is mighty purty, but he smokes so much ez it is, I don't know ez I want to encourage him. Besides, it seems a waste o' money to buy a Christmus gif' thet a person has to lay aside when company comes in, an' a silver-mounted pipe ain't no politer to smoke in the presence o' ladies than a corncob is. An' ez for when we're by ourselves—shucks.

"Ef you don't mind, Mr. Lawson, I'll stroll around through the sto'e an' see what you've got while you wait on some o' them thet know their own minds. I know mine well enough. *What*

N 193

I want is *that swingin' ice-pitcher,* an' my judgment tells me thet they ain't a more suitable present in yo' sto'e for a settled man thet has built hisself a residence au' furnished it complete the way *he* has, but of co'se 'twouldn't never do. I always think how I'd enjoy it when the minister called. I wonder what Mr. Lawson thinks o' me back here a-talkin' to myself. I always like to talk about the things I'm buyin'. That's a mighty fine saddle-blanket, indeed it is. He was talkin' about a new saddle-blanket the other day. But that's a thing a person could pick up almost any day, a saddle-blanket is. A' ice-pitcher now—

"Say, Mr. Lawson, lemme look at that tiltin'-pitcher again, please, sir. I jest want to see ef the spout is gold-lined. Yes, so it is—an' little holes down in the throat of it, too. It cert'n'y is well made, it cert'n'y is. I s'pose them holes is to strain out grasshoppers or anything thet might fall into it. That musician thet choked to death at the barbecue down at Pump.Springs last summer might 'a' been livin' yet ef they'd had sech ez this to pass water in, instid o' that open pail. *He's* got a mighty keerless way o' drinkin' out o' open dippers, too. No tellin' what he'll scoop up some day. They'd be great safety for him in a pitcher like this—ef I could only make him see it. It would seem a sort o' awkward thing to pack out to the well every single time, an' he won't drink no water but what he draws fresh. An' I s'pose it would look sort o' silly to put it in here jest to drink it out again.

"Sir? Oh yes, I saw them saddle-bags hangin' up back there, an' they are fine, mighty fine, ez you say, an' his are purty near wo'e out, but lordy, I don't want to buy a Christmus gif' thet's hung up in the harness - room half the time. What's that you say? Won't you all never git done a-runnin' me about that side-saddle? You can't pleg me about that. I got it for his pleasure, ef it was for my use, an', come to think about it, I'd be jest reversin' the thing on the pitcher. It would be for his use an' my pleasure. I wish I could see my way to buy it for him. Both goblets go with it, you say—an' the slop bowl? It cert'n'y is handsome—it cert'n'y is. An' it's expensive—nobody could accuse me o' stintin' 'im. Wonder why they didn't put some polar bears on the goblets, too. They'd 'a' had to be purty small bears, but they could 'a' been cubs, easy.

"I don't reely believe, Mr. Lawson, indeed I don't, thet I could find a mo' suitable present for him ef I took a month, an' I don't keer what he's

a-pickin' out for me this minute, it can't be no
handsomer 'n this. Th' ain't no use—I'll haf to
have it—for 'im. Jest charge it, please, an' now
I want it marked. I'll pay cash for the markin',
out of my egg money. An' I want his full name.
Have it stamped on the iceberg right beside the
bear. 'Ephraim N. Trimble.' No, you needn't
to spell out the middle name. I should say not.
Ef you knew what it was you wouldn't ask me.
Why, it's Nebuchadnezzar. It 'd use up the
whole iceberg. Besides, I couldn't never think
o' Nebuchadnezzar there an' not a spear o' grass
on the whole lan'scape. You needn't to laugh.
I know it's silly, but I always think o' sech ez
that. No, jest write it, 'Ephraim N. Trimble,
from his wife, Kitty.' Be sure to put in the
Kitty, so in after years it'll show which wife
give it to him. Of co'se, them thet knew us
both would know which one. Mis' Mary Jane
wouldn't never have approved of it in the world.
Why, she used to rip up her old crocheted tidies
an' things an' use 'em over in bastin' thread, so
they tell me. She little dremp' who she was
a-savin' for, poor thing. She was buyin' this
pitcher then, but she didn't know it. But I
keep a-runnin' on. Go on with the inscription,
Mr. Lawson. What have you got? 'From his

wife, Kitty'—what's the matter with 'affectionate wife'? You say affectionate is a purty expensive word? But 'lovin'' 'll do jest ez well, an' it comes cheaper, you say? An' plain 'wife' comes cheapest of all? An' I don't know but what it's mo' suitable, anyhow—at his age. Of co'se, you must put in the date, an' make the 'Kitty' nice an' fancy, please. Lordy, well, the deed's done—an' I reckon he'll threaten to divo'ce me when he sees it—till he reads the inscription. Better put in the 'lovin',' I reckon, an' put it in capitals— they don't cost no more, do they? Well, good-bye, Mr. Lawson, I reckon you'll be glad to see me go. I've outstayed every last one thet was here when I come. Well, good-bye! Have it marked immejiate, please, an' I'll call back in an hour. Good-bye, again!"

Part III

WHEN old man Trimble stood before the fire-place at midnight that night, stuffing little parcels into the deep, borrowed stocking, he chuckled noiselessly, and glanced with affection towards the corner of the room where his young wife lay sleeping. He was a fat old man, and

197

as he stood with shaking sides in his loose, home-made pajamas, he would have done credit to a more conscious impersonation of old Santa himself.

His task finally done, he glanced down at a tall bundle that stood on the floor almost immediately in front of him, moved back with his hands resting on his hips, and thoughtfully surveyed it.

"Well, ef anybody had 'a' told it on me I never would 'a' believed it," he said, under his breath. "The idee o' me, Ephe Trimble, settin' up sech a thing ez that in his house—at my time o' life." Then, glancing towards the sleeper, he added, with a chuckle, "an' ef they'd 'a' prophesied it I wouldn't 'a' believed sech ez *thet*, neither—at my time o' life—bless her little curly head."

He sat down on the floor beside the bundle, clipped the twine, and cautiously pushed back the wrappings. Then, rising, he carefully set each piece of the water-set up above the stocking on the mantel. He did not stop to examine it. He was anxious to get it in place without noise.

It made a fine show, even in the dim, unsteady light of the single taper that burned in its tumbler of oil close beside the bed. Indeed, when it arose in all its splendor, he was very much impressed.

"A thing like that ought to have a chandelier to set it off right," he thought—"yas, and she'll have one, too—she'll have anything she wants—thet I can give her."

Sleep came slowly to the old man that night, and even long after his eyes were closed, the silver things seemed arrayed in line upon his mental retina. And when, after a long while, he fell into a troubled slumber, it was only to dream. And in his dream old Judge Robinson's mother-in-law seemed to come and stand before him—black dress, side curls, and all—and when he looked at her for the first time in his life unabashed—she began to bow, over and over again, and to say with each salutation, "Be seated "—"be seated "—"be seated," getting farther and farther away with each bow until she was a mere speck in the distance—and then the speck became a spot of white, and he saw that the old lady had taken on a spout and a handle, and that she was only an ice-pitcher, tilting, and tilting, and tilting—while from the yellow spout came a fine metallic voice saying, "Be seated "—"be seated"—again and again.

Then there would be a change. Two ladies
would appear approaching each other and re-
treating—turning into two ice-pitchers, tilting
to each other, then passing from tilting pitchers
to bowing ladies, until sometimes there seemed
almost to be a pitcher and a lady in view at the
same time. When he began to look for them
both at once the dream became tantalizing.
Twin ladies and twin pitchers—but never quite
clearly a lady and a pitcher. Even while the
vision tormented him it held him fast—perhaps
because he was tired, having lost his first hours
of sleep.

He was still sleeping soundly, spite of the dis-
solving views of the novel panorama, when above
the two voices that kept inviting him to "be
seated," there arose, in muffled tones at first,
and then with distressing distinctness, a sound
of sobbing. It made the old man turn on his
pillow even while he slept, for it was the voice
of a woman, and he was tender of heart. It
seemed in the dream and yet not of it—this
awful, suppressed sobbing that disturbed his
slumber, but was not quite strong enough to
break it. But presently, instead of the muffled
sob, there came a cumulative outburst, like that
of a too hard-pressed turkey-gobbler forced to

the wall. He thought it was the old black gobbler at first, and he even said, "Shoo," as he sprang from his bed. But a repetition of the sound sent him bounding through the open door into the dining-room, dazed and trembling.

Seated beside the dining-table there, with her head buried in her arms, sat his little wife. Before her, ranged in line upon the table, stood the silver water-set—her present to him. He was beside her in a moment—leaning over her, his arms about her shoulders.

"Why, honey," he exclaimed, "what on earth—"

At this she only cried the louder. There was no further need for restraint. The old man scratched his head. He was very much distressed.

"Why, honey," he repeated, "tell its old man all about it. Didn't it like the purty pitcher thet its old husband bought for it? Was it too big—or too little—or too heavy for it to tote all the way out here from that high mantel? Why didn't it wake up its lazy ol' man and make him pack it out here for it?"

It was no use. She was crying louder than ever. He did not know what to do. He began to be cold and he saw that she was shivering.

There was no fire in the dining-room. He must do something. "Tell its old man what it would 'a' ruther had," he whispered in her ear, "jest tell him, ef it don't like its pitcher—"

At this she made several efforts to speak, her voice breaking in real turkey-gobbler sobs each time, but finally she managed to wail:

"It ain't m-m-m-mi-i-i-ne!"

"Not yours! Why, honey. What can she mean? Did it think I bought it for anybody else? Ain't yours! Well, I like that. Lemme fetch that lamp over here till you read the writin' on the side of it, an' I'll show you whose it is." He brought the lamp.

"Read that, now. Why, honey! Wh—wh—wh—what in thunder an' lightnin'! They've done gone an' reversed it. The fool's put my name first—'Ephraim N. Trimble. From—his—'

"Why, Jerusalem jinger!

"No wonder she thought I was a low-down dog—to buy sech a thing an' mark it in my own name—no wonder—here on Christmus, too. The idee o' Rowton not seein' to it thet it was done right—"

By this time the little woman had somewhat recovered herself. Still, she stammered fearfully.

"R-r-r-owton ain't never s-s-s-saw that pitcher. It come from L-l-l-awson's, d-d-down at Washin'ton, an' I b-bought it for y-y-y-you !"

"Why, honey—darlin'—" A sudden light came into the old man's eyes. He seized the lamp and hurried to the door of the bed-chamber, and looked in. This was enough. Perhaps it was mean—but he could not help it—he set the lamp down on the table, dropped into a chair, and fairly howled with laughter.

"No wonder I dremp' ol' Mis' Meredy was twins!" he screamed. "Why, h-h-honey," he was nearly splitting his old sides—"why, honey, I ain't seen a thing but these two swingin' pitchers all night. They've been dancin' before me —them an' what seemed like a pair o' ol' Mis' Meredys, an' between 'em all I ain't slep' a wink."

"N-n-either have I. An' I dremp' about ol' Mis' M-m-m-eredy, too. I dremp' she had come to live with us—an' thet y-y-you an' me had moved into the back o' the house. That's why I got up. I couldn't sleep easy, an' I thought I might ez well git up an' see wh-wh-what you'd brought me. But I didn't no mor'n glance at it. But you can't say you didn't sleep, for you was a-s-s-snorin' when I come out here—"

"An' so was you, honey, when I 'ranged them things on the mantel. Lemme go an' git the other set an' compare 'em. That one I picked out is mighty purty."

"I'll tell you befo' you fetch 'em thet they're exactly alike"—she began to cry again—"even to the p-p-polar bear. I saw that at a glance, an' it makes it s-s-so much more ridic'—"

"Hush, honey. I'm reely ashamed of you—I reely am. Seems to me ef they're jest alike, so much the better. What's the matter with havin' a pair of 'em ? We might use one for butter-milk."

"Th-that would be perfectly ridiculous. A polar bear'd look like a fool on a buttermilk pitcher. N-n-no, the place for pitchers like them is in halls, on tables, where anybody comin' in can see 'em an' stop an' git a drink. They couldn't be nothin' tackier'n pourin' buttermilk out of a' ice-pitcher."

"Of co'se, if you say so, we won't—I jest thought maybe—or, I tell you what we might do. I could easy take out a panel o' banisters out of the side po'ch, an' put in a pair o' stair-steps, so ez to make a sort o' side entrance to the house, an' we could set one of 'em in *it*. I would make the pitcher come a little high, of co'se, but it would set off that side o' the house lovely, an' ef you say so—

"Lemme go git 'em all out here together."

As he trudged in presently loaded up with the duplicate set he said, "I wonder ef you know what time it is, wife ?"

She glanced over her shoulder at the clock on the wall.

"Don't look at that. It's six o'clock last night by that. I forgot to wind her up. No. It's half-past three o'clock—that's all it is." By this time he had placed his water-set beside hers upon the table. "Why, honey," he exclaimed, "where on earth ? I don't see a sign of a' inscription on this—an' what is this paper in the spout ? Here, you read it, wife, I ain't got my specs."

"'Too busy to mark to-day—send back after Christmas —sorry.   RowTon.'"

"Why, it—an' here's another paper. What can this be, I wonder ?"

"'To my darling wife, from her affectionate husband.'"

The little wife colored as she read it.

"Oh, that ain't nothin' but the motter he was to print on it. But ain't it lucky thet he didn't do it? I'll change it—that's what I'll do—for anything you say. There, now. Don't that fix it?"

She was very still for a moment—very thoughtful. "An' affectionate is a mighty expensive word, too," she said, slowly, glancing over the intended inscription, in her husband's handwriting. "Yes. Your pitcher don't stand for a thing but generosity—an' mine don't mean a thing but selfishness. Yes, take it back, cert'nly, that is ef you'll get me anything I want for it. Will you?"

"Shore. They's a cow-topped butter-dish an' no end o' purty little things out there you might like. An' ef it's goin' back, it better be a-goin'. I can ride out to town an' back befo' breakfast. Come, kiss me, wife."

She threw both arms around her old husband's neck, and kissed him on one cheek and then on the other. Then she kissed his lips. And then, as she went for pen and paper, she said: "Hurry, now, an' hitch up, an' I'll be writin' down what I want in exchange—an' you can put it in yo' pocket."

In a surprisingly short time the old man was on his way—a heaped basket beside him, a tiny bit of writing in his pocket. When he had turned into the road he drew rein for a moment, lit a match, and this is what he read :

"My dear Husband,—I want one silver-mounted brier-wood pipe and a smoking set—a nice lava one—and I want a set of them fine overhauls like them that Mis Pope give Mr. Pope that time I said she was too extravagant, and if they's any money left over I want some nice tobacco, the best. I want all the price of the ice-set took up. even to them affectionate words they never put on.

"Your affectionate and loving wife,

"Kitty."

When Ephraim put the little note back in his pocket, he took out his handkerchief and wiped his eyes.

Her good neighbors and friends, even as far as Simpkinsville and Washington, had their little jokes over Mis' Trimble's giving her splendor-despising husband a swinging ice-pitcher, but they never knew of the two early trips of the twin pitcher, nor of the midnight comedy in the Trimble home.

But the old man often recalls it, and as he sits in his front hall smoking his silver-mounted pipe, and shaking its ashes into the lava bowl that stands beside the ice-pitcher at his elbow, he sometimes chuckles to himself.

Noticing his shaking shoulders as he sat thus

one day his wife turned from the window, where she stood watering her geraniums, and said :

"What on earth are you a-laughin' at, honey?" (She often calls him "honey" now.)

"How did you know I was a-laughin' ?" He looked over his shoulder at her as he spoke.

"Why, I seen yo' shoulders a-shakin'—that's how." And then she added, with a laugh, "An' now I see yo' reflection in the side o' the ice-pitcher, with a zig-zag grin on you a mile long—yo' smile just happened to strike a iceberg."

He chuckled again.

"Is that so ? Well, the truth is, I'm just sort o' tickled over things in general, an' I'm a-settin' here gigglin', jest from pure contentment."

A MINOR CHORD

A MINOR CHORD

I AM an old bachelor, and I live alone in my corner upper room of an ancient house of *Chambres garnies*, down on the lower edge of the French quarter of New Orleans.

When I made my nest here, forty years ago, I felt myself an old man, and the building was even then a dilapidated old rookery, and since then we—the house and I—have lapsed physically with the decline of the neighborhood about us, until now our only claims to gentility are perhaps our memories and our reserves.

The habit of introspection formed by so isolated an existence tends to develop morbid views of life, and throws one out of sympathetic relations with the world of progress, we are told; but is there not some compensation for this in the acquisition of finer and more subtle perception of things hidden from the social, laughing, hurrying world ? So it seems to me, and even though the nicer discernment bring pain, as it often does—as all refinement must—who would yield it for a grosser content resulting from a duller vision ?

To contemplate the procession that passes daily beneath my window, with its ever-shifting pictures of sorrow, of decrepitude ill-matched with want, new motherhood, and mendicancy, with uplifted eye and palm—to look down upon all this with only a passing sigh, as my worthy but material fat landlady does, would imply a spiritual blindness infinitely worse than the pang which the keener perception induces.

There are in this neighborhood of moribund pretensions a few special objects which strike a note of such sadness in my heart that the most exquisite pain ensues—a pain which seems almost bodily, such as those for which we take physic ; yet I could never confuse it with the neuralgic dart which it so nearly resembles, so closely does it follow the sight or sound which I know induces it.

There is a young lawyer who passes twice a day beneath my window. . . . I say he is young, for all the moving world is young to me, at eighty

—and yet he seems old at five-and-forty, for his temples are white.

I know this man's history. The only son of a proud house, handsome, gifted—even somewhat of a poet in his youth — he married a soulless woman, who began the ruin which the wine-cup finished. It is an old story. In a mad hour he forged another man's name—then, a wanderer on the face of the earth, he drifted about with never a local habitation or a name, until his aged father had made good the price of his honor, when he came home — "tramped home," the world says — and, now, after years of variable steadiness, he has built upon the wreck of his early life a sort of questionable confidence which brings him half-averted recognition; and every day, with the gray always glistening on his temples and the clear profile of the past outlining itself—though the high-bred face is low between the shoulders now—he passes beneath my window with halting step to and from the old courthouse, where, by virtue of his father's position, he holds a minor office.

Almost within a stone's throw of my chamber this man and his aged father — the latter now a hopeless paralytic—live together in the ruins of their old home.

MORIAH'S MOURNING

Year by year the river, by constant cavings, has swallowed nearly all its extensive grounds, yet beyond the low-browed Spanish cottage that clings close within the new levee, "the ghost of a garden" fronts the river. Here, amid broken marbles—lyreless Apollos, Pegasus bereft of wings, and prostrate Muses—the hardier roses, golden-rod, and honeysuckle run riot within the old levee, between the comings of the waters that at intervals steal in and threaten to swallow all at a gulp.

The naked old house, grotesquely guarded by the stately skeleton of a moss-grown oak, is thus bereft, by the river in front and the public road at its back, of all but the bare fact of survival.

No visitor ever enters here; but in the summer evenings two old men may be seen creeping with difficult steps from its low portal up to the brow of the bank, where they sit in silence and watch the boats go by.

The picture is not devoid of pathos, and even the common people whisper together as they look upon the figures of father and son sitting in the moonlight; and no one likes to pass the door at night, for there are grewsome tales of ghosts afloat, in which decapitated statues are said to stalk about the old garden at nightfall.

A MINOR CHORD

A sigh always escapes me as I look upon this desolate scene ; but it is not now, but when the old - young man, the son, passes my door each day, carrying in his pale hands a bunch of flowers which he keeps upon his desk in the little back office, that my mysterious pain possesses me.

Why does this hope - forsaken man carry a bunch of flowers ? Is it the surviving poet within him that finds companionship in them, or does he seem to see in their pure hearts, as in a mirror, a reflection of his own sinless youth ?

These questions I cannot answer ; but every day, as he passes with the flowers, I follow him with fascinated eye until he is quite lost in the distance, my heart rent the while with this incisive pain.

Finally, he is lost to view. The dart passes through and out my breast, and, as I turn, my eye falls upon a pretty rose-garden across the way, where live a mother and her two daughters.

. . . .

Seventeen years ago this woman's husband— the father—went away and never returned. The daughters are grown, and they are poor. The elder performs some clerical work up in Canal Street, and I love to watch her trig little figure come and go—early and late.

The younger, who is fairer, has a lover, and the two sit together on a little wrought-iron bench, or gather roses from the box-bordered beds in the small inland garden, which lies behind the moss-grown wall and battened gate; and sometimes the mother comes out and smiles upon the pair.

The mother is a gentlewoman, and though she wears a steel thimble with an open top, like a tailor's, and her finger is pricked with the needle, she walks and smiles, even waters her roses, with a lady's grace; but it seems to me that the pretty pink daughter's lover is less a gentleman than this girl's lover should be — less than her grandfather must have been when he courted her grandmother in this same rose-garden—less than this maid's lover would be if her father had not gone to India, and her mother did not sew seams for a living.

As I sit and watch this peaceful fragment of a family, my heart seems to find repose in its apparent content; but late at night, when the lover has gone and the mother and daughters are asleep, when I rise to close my shutters I perceive, between the parted curtains in the mother's window, a light dimly burning. When I see this beacon in the deserted wife's chamber, and remember that I have seen it burning there, like the faint but steadfast hope that refuses to be extinguished, for seventeen years, the pain of pains comes into my heart.

. . . .

There is a little old man with a hump upon his shoulder who passes often in the crowd, and a sight of him always awakens this pain within me.

It is not the tragedy of senility which his extreme age pictures, nor yet the hump upon his back, which stirs my note of pain.

Years ago this man left his wife, for a price, to another who had betrayed her, and disappeared from the scene of his ignominy. When the woman was dead and her betrayer gone, the husband came back, an old man ; and now, as I see him bending beneath its weight, the hump upon his shoulder seems to be labelled with this price which, in my imagination, though originally the bag of gold, has by a slow and chemically unexplained process of ossification, become a part of himself, and will grotesquely deform his skeleton a hundred years to come. When, morning and evening, I see this old man trudge laboriously, staggering always towards the left, down the street, until he disappears in the clump of willows that overshadow the cemetery gate, and

I know that he is going for a lonely vigil to the grave of the dishonored woman, his lost wife, pain, keen as a Damascus blade, enters my heart.

. . . .

I close my window and come in, for the night dews are falling and I am rheumatic and stiff in the legs.

So, every night, musing, I go early to my bed, but before I lie down, after my prayer is said, I rise to put fresh water in the vase of flowers, which are always fresh, beneath the picture upon my wall.

For one moment I stand and gaze into a pure, girlish face, with a pallid brow and far-away blue eyes.

She was only fifteen years old, and I twice as many, when we quarrelled like foolish children.

The day she married my brother—my youngest, best-beloved brother Benjamin—I laid this miniature, face downward, in a secret drawer of my desk.

In the first year she died, and in another Benjamin had taken to himself a new wife, with merrier eyes and ruddier lips.

My heart leaped within me when I kissed my new sister, but she knew not that my joy was because she was giving me back my love.

A MINOR CHORD

Trembling with ecstasy, I took this image from its hiding-place, and for nearly fifty years the flowers beneath it have not withered.

As I stood alone here one night, ere I knew he had entered, my little brother's hand was upon my shoulder. For a moment only he was silent, awe-stricken.

" She was always yours, my brother," he said, presently, in a tremulous whisper. "I did not know until it was too late. She had misunderstood—but God was very merciful," and turning he left her to me.

And still each day I lay fresh flowers at her shrine, cherishing the dart that rends my heart the while, for its testimony to the immortality of my passion.

Do you smile because a trembling old man feasts his failing eyes on a fair woman's face and prates of love and flowers and beauty ? Smile if you will, but if you do it is because you, being of the earth, cannot understand.

These things are of the spirit ; and palsy and rheumatism and waning strength are of the flesh, which profiteth nothing.

THE END